Ely Echoes

The Portages Grow Longer

Written and illustrated by Bob Cary

Pfeifer-Hamilton

Duluth, Minnesota

Portions of this book first appeared in the *Senior Reporter* and the *Ely Echo.*

Pfeifer-Hamilton Publishers
210 W Michigan
Duluth MN 55802-1908
218-727-0500
www.phpublisher.com

Ely Echoes: The Portages Grow Longer

Printed in the United States of America by Versa Press, Inc.
10 9 8 7 6 5 4 3 2 1

Cover Art: Bob Cary
Art Director: Joy Morgan Dey
Editorial Director: Heather Isernhagen

Library of Congress Cataloging-in-Publication Data
Cary, Bob.
    Ely echoes : the portages grow longer / written and illustrated
by Bob Cary.
     192 p. 23 cm.
   "Portions of this book first appeared in the Senior Reporter and
the Ely Echo."
  ISBN 1-57025-200-9
  1. Ely (Minn.)—Social life and customs. 2. Ely (Minn.)
Biography. 3. Country life—Minnesota—Ely. 4. Cary, Bob. 5. Cary,
Bob—Friends and associates. I. Title.
  F614.E4 C37 2000
  977.6'77—dc21
  [B]
                                                99-6706
                                                CIP

Dedication

Books do not simply happen. Nor are they the effort of one person. Books require a team effort and I wish to acknowledge some members of the team that assembled this book. First, there is my wife, Edie, who has fished, hunted, and paddled the bow of our canoe the year and a half we have been married. Don Tubesing, publisher of Pfeifer-Hamilton, who first suggested the idea for this book, and Heather Isernhagen, also of Pfeifer-Hamilton, who helped to assemble and organize the material.

And I am most grateful to Anne Swenson, owner and publisher of the *Ely Echo* newspaper who retrieved much of the material from our files and put it on a computer disk for subsequent use. And one more nod, to Larry Fortner, publisher of the *Senior Reporter* in Duluth, Minnesota, for allowing the use of reprints from his publication. There are no doubt many others who should get credit, but I am more than three-quarters of a century old and simply cannot remember. No today. Tomorrow I will remember. Forgive me.

Contents

Foreword

My wife, Edie, and I live in the forest adjacent to Moose Lake, twenty-two miles east of Ely, where we enjoy the bounty of woods and water, savoring deer and grouse, walleye, bass, trout, and panfish. This bounty we share with our neighbors, including timber wolves, bears, otters, hawks, eagles, and ospreys. Spring, summer, and fall, we paddle the canoes trails and walk the portages. In winter, we travel much of the same area, but on skis or snowshoes. In all of this, we have developed a profound appreciation for this wild country and for its former tenants, the Ojibwe people. Indeed, it is their lakes, their portages, and even canoes and snowshoes of their design we use to get around. And it is their philosophy we live by, of having a reverence for the handiwork of the Great Spirit and of meeting life's challenges with a smile. Along the world's byways, over the last seventy-seven years, this writer has had the good fortune to meet hundreds of wonderful people, all of whom had a story, all of whom had something to teach. Some of the more colorful are included in this narrative for your pleasure.

Bob Cary
1999

Introduction

Looking back on over three-fourths a century of life, I am aware that luck exerts a considerable influence on survival. Everyone experiences luck, either good or bad. Given the choice, one is best advised to select the good variety. Mine has largely been good, far better than deserved. In the course of events, rather early to be sure, a Guardian Angel made a fortunate appearance in my life.

This patient and suffering Angel did not keep me from doing a lot of dumb things, but it did keep me from utter destruction. It got me through a number of childhood diseases; saw me through the trauma of grade school; puberty; and three years, eight months, and fourteen days of World War II; and ushered me into the field of journalism, from whence I have labored more or less diligently for these last fifty years. My Guardian Angel provided me with Lillian, my talented and fun-loving wife of forty-six years; two daughters; and the opportunity to migrate to Ely, Minnesota, and extract a living on the rim of the incredible Boundary Waters Canoe Area Wilderness.

On June 11, 1993, cancer took my wife. On October 9, 1996, my friend and neighbor, Dr. Robert Sommer, died of a heart condition. For fifteen years, Robert, his wife, Edith, Lillian, and I had camped, canoed, hunted, and gone to crosscountry ski races together. Of that foursome, Edith and I were all that was left.

On February 21, 1998, that same Guardian Angel brought Edith and me together in marriage at the University Methodist Church in Duluth. Upon reflection, we have a strong suspicion that our Angel may not necessarily be of the conventional type.

Possibly even a trifle quirky. Indeed, when you have a groom who is seventy-seven years old and a bride of sixty-five, a certain amount of mirth must of necessity be associated with the occasion. Like two vintage cars, we are certainly well over warranty, functioning on well-worn and largely nonreplaceable parts. After an aggregate of eighty-nine years marriage to other spouses, our newly adjusted life together has been largely one of unlimited laughter.

The three of us, with a measure of optimism, thus embark upon whatever the future holds: Edith, myself, and that wonderful Guardian Angel, who is still around and decidedly in business. And in this book, we would like to take you along on some of our adventures.

Genesis

Few of us remember much about the first couple of years we were on earth. No one ever says they recall being born although apparently we all were. Memory usually begins a few years later. I can recall two incidents from 1924, when I was three. The first was a ride in a canoe, a long, green craft that belonged to my Aunt Nell and that she kept at her summer cottage on the Fox River. Two of my older cousins took me for a ride, allowing me to sit on the varnished wooden floorboards in the center. My nose, I recall, came just to the gunwales, and I noted the water moving past, the green shoreline, and the smell of the river. Not much else. Oh yes. There were some dragonflies following the canoe, and I distinctly remember being told that these were "Devil's Darning Needles" and were apt to sew our mouths shut. I kept both hands over my mouth.

The other memory from age three is my first fishing trip with my father. This was somewhat of a desperation deal on his part, as my mother explained years later. Apparently, as my father was gathering up his boots and tackle to head for the DuPage River, I put up an ear-splitting protest.

"Wanna go fissin'," I screamed, or something in that vein.

Ely Echoes

My mother, to terminate the uproar, sided with me and insisted my father take me along. This he reluctantly did, no doubt with considerable distaste and apprehension. The part I remember most was arriving at the river, a clear, lily-lined bass stream, and waiting for something to happen. I knew we were going fishing, although I was not certain what that was. Dad assembled his tackle, then rigged me up with an old tubular steel rod, a reel, a hook, sinker, and bobber. He jammed a squirming nightcrawler on the hook, a wriggling, reddish brown invertebrate, carried me to a big boulder that split the current in midstream, and deposited me thereupon. He cast out the bait, jammed the rod into my hands, and instructed me to stay put and under no circumstances to let go of the rod.

Then dad waded slowly downstream in his hip boots, drifting his line ahead in the current. The next part is unclear in my mind, but dad said he had proceeded perhaps twenty feet when he heard a gurgle and a cough behind. He glanced back to see most of my head sticking out of the water, eyes wide with terror, the fishing rod clenched in my right hand. Apparently, rather than stay on the boulder, I opted to wade downstream, too. Indeed, my father liked to say later that this was an indication of how little I would pay attention to anything he said throughout much of my life.

In any event, dad plucked me dripping and bawling from the river, waded to the bank, and assessed the situation. It was obvious that there was no earthly way he could do any serious angling with this squalling, dripping urchin in tow. Fortunately, it was a warm, sunshiny day, and dad removed my shirt and pants, wrung them out, and put them back on me. We did fish a little from the bank, without result, while the hot sun eliminated some of my dampness. The only other thing I recall is that dad drove to a roadside cafe, where he bought us each a beef barbecue and a bottle of white soda pop.

With negotiations thus opened, he insisted several times that I promise not to tell my mother that I slid off the boulder and wound up in the river. And I never did.

By age six, I was an old hand at fishing. Many Sundays, after church, we drove to Aunt Nell's white frame cottage on the Fox River. Nell was a grade-school teacher who spent the summer vacation period at the cottage, which became sort of a Sunday afternoon gathering place for a number of relatives and acquaintances. The adults usually played bridge or pinochle; the older kids took canoe rides. Mainly, I went fishing. The Fox River in those days ran clear and cool, haven for a significant population of bass, sunfish, and rock bass. I fished from shore. I fished from Aunt Nell's dock. I fished from every dock upstream and downstream I could walk to. My luck was erratic, but occasionally I captured a number of fish, mostly small, which wound up in a bucket I carried. At length, I headed back to the cottage to display my catch, however meager, and watched intently while dad dressed out and scaled the fish. The sense of accomplishment was complete when Aunt Nell fried the fish to a crisp brown in hot butter and we ate them. Each of us got perhaps a mouthful, but I don't remember anyone ever disparaging the fish as being too small. Out of consideration for my age, they praised my efforts.

Certainly there were lessons to be learned in these exercises. One, that if a person expended a determined effort in a worthy enterprise such as angling, the result might be worthwhile. The idea of catch and release, of putting fish unharmed back into the water, was not yet a part of my comprehension. Fish were caught to eat. In these later decades of my life, when I have been fortunate enough to pursue the sport in some of the premier wilderness waters of North America, most of the fish caught have been carefully released.

However, we often select a fish or two for dinner, and therein lies another lesson. Those who aspire in life to amass great wealth, becoming millionaires or even billionaires, may not, in any gourmet supper club at any price, partake of finer fare than pan-browned walleye fillets, poached bass, baked trout, or a chowder of pike, freshly caught and prepared at lakeside. Indeed, the very wealthy, unless they take time off to capture their own, are doubtless eating fish caught by someone else in some distance place, fish that are not nearly as fresh nor as fine eating as the ones caught by those of us with considerably smaller financial standing . . . or perhaps none at all.

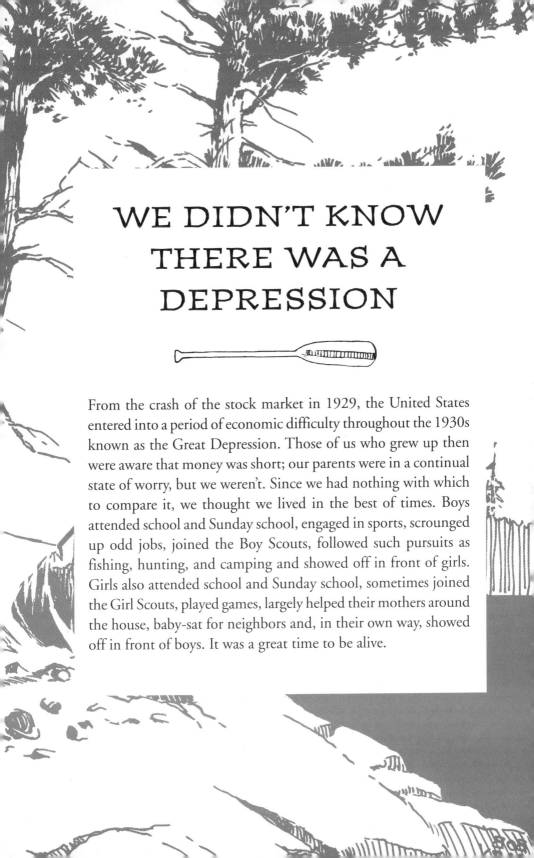

WE DIDN'T KNOW THERE WAS A DEPRESSION

From the crash of the stock market in 1929, the United States entered into a period of economic difficulty throughout the 1930s known as the Great Depression. Those of us who grew up then were aware that money was short; our parents were in a continual state of worry, but we weren't. Since we had nothing with which to compare it, we thought we lived in the best of times. Boys attended school and Sunday school, engaged in sports, scrounged up odd jobs, joined the Boy Scouts, followed such pursuits as fishing, hunting, and camping and showed off in front of girls. Girls also attended school and Sunday school, sometimes joined the Girl Scouts, played games, largely helped their mothers around the house, baby-sat for neighbors and, in their own way, showed off in front of boys. It was a great time to be alive.

Magical Summers

As some of us grow older, we inevitably find ourselves recalling the happier times of our youth. Perhaps magical times. In recent years, my thoughts go back to summers spent at the river cottage owned by my maiden aunt, Nell Patterson. A school teacher nine months of the year, Nellie migrated each summer to her white frame retreat on the river, where she could study and read. During the Depression, my father and mother were not opposed to having one less mouth to feed, a rather ravenous mouth at that; thus I was farmed out to Aunt Nell as her handyman, wood splitter, water hauler, and all-around gofer.

What glorious summers those were. There was kindling to split on a wood block in the shade of huge elms. Countless gallons of icy cold, clear water had to be pumped by hand from the well. Repairs had to be made on the plank steps to the river and to the rustic boat dock. A fresh layer of green enamel was applied to the flat-bottom rowboat and to the sleek eighteen-foot Old Town canoe, a watercraft that did as much to shape my life as the nine months spent in school. The canoe was my transportation to the village some two miles distant, where groceries and other supplies were purchased.

In the golden mists of many mornings, I would quietly pole that wood-and-canvas craft upstream through riffle and pool like voyageurs of old, marking the flush of mallards, teal, snipe, and bitterns. At times, I paused to watch gaunt blue herons and white egrets, poised motionless on one leg, ambushing minnows in the shoals. Bills extended, eyes focused, they would wait with infinite patience, then strike with blinding speed, spearing tiny fish, raising them vertically, and swallowing them with one gulp.

Dragonflies were given wide berth because I was sure these "Devil's Darning Needles" could sew one's mouth shut. Turtles plopped into the current from their sun porches on shoreline logs, and there appeared the occasional swirl of a feeding bass. Overall was the pungency of drying mud mingled with the scent of sweet clover, wild irises, and wild rose. A background a cappella chorus of red-winged blackbirds, meadowlarks, flickers, and robins filled the air.

All I wore was a pair of pants. Barebacked and barefoot, I reveled in the sun's warmth, the serenity of the largely uninhabited shoreline, as I poled upstream. In the village, I tied up the canoe, padded barefoot to the counter of the grocery store, handed over my list of necessities, and paid the bill in cash. Usually, Aunt Nellie allowed an extra nickel for a strawberry ice-cream cone, which I carefully savored as the canoe bore me silently back toward the cottage.

Vespers at dark were provided by the cry of nighthawks or the wail of a tiny screech owl tucked away on a nearby oak. Reveille at dawn was sounded by the clank of cowbells as the herd from the farm above was called in for the morning milking.

In memory, I can hear, see, and smell all the magic. It is almost as though I am there again. Perhaps one day I shall be.

Happy Birthday, George

The large, framed print on the wall of Miss Ream's sixth-grade class was the same familiar portrait of George Washington recognized on one-dollar bills. All members of Taft Grade School Class of 1933 knew February 22 was Washington's birthday, a national holiday, and our esteem for the nation's first president was measurably enhanced by the fact that there was no school on that day.

It is doubtful that Miss Ream would have evinced any enthusiasm for something as nebulous as "President's Day," a relatively recent designation to include political figures of somewhat lesser stature. Nonetheless, on the days leading up to Washington's birthday, Miss Ream regularly entertained us with stories of the American Revolution, from time to time aiming a finger at the portrait. Through high school, into college, and beyond, Miss Ream's students carried with them a love of history and an appreciation for the founders of our nation.

Thus it was that this winter my wife, Edith, and I stood upon the British ramparts at Yorktown, Virginia, and gazed with a feeling of awe at the battlefield where Washington's forces in 1781 defeated the scarlet-jacketed troops of General Lord Cornwallis,

effectively freeing the colonies from British rule. The National Park Service has done a remarkable job of preserving the remains of the massive earthworks Cornwallis felt were impregnable. Cannon muzzles projecting from embrasures were aimed at American and French forces forming in the woods and fields to the east.

Significantly, the 7,300 core veterans of Washington's force had marched 450 miles from the siege at New York to lead the Yorktown attack. Letters and journal accounts written by some of those men relate in graphic detail the bitter hardships endured by the Colonial troops through five years of combat, five years of inadequate food, tattered uniforms, and near-nonexistent pay.

Starting as a ragtag army with mostly inexperienced officers, the Colonials were often defeated and mostly on the run. But through it all, from buck private to regimental commander, there was a staunch belief in the cause of freedom and an unwavering faith in their commander-in-chief. There was something about this man, his courage, his determination, his cool bearing in battle that evoked unwavering devotion not only from his own troops but from the 7,000 French allies under General Rochambeau and the French fleet of Admiral DeGrasse.

Cornwallis's position around Yorktown, however, appeared impregnable. Even today, a visitor can see how the two strong points, No. 9 and No. 10, anchoring the British east flank on the York River, could lay a devastating fire on any attackers. Washington, perhaps relying on his experience in the French and Indian War, ordered what may have been the first American commando raid. In the dark of night, with unloaded muskets to preserve silence, 400 crack Yankees and 400 veteran French troops stormed Redoubts 9 and 10 with bayonets, decimating the British forces. With this loss and with his left flank unprotected, Cornwallis's position became untenable. Five days later the chagrined British army marched in column, to the sound of fife and drum, to a field surrounded by the French and American forces, where they hurled their muskets to the ground in surrender.

The Visitor Center, operated by the Park Service, provides displays of artifacts from that battle, a film with actors portraying the events at Yorktown, a replica of a British war sloop, and numerous books and pamphlets relating to the battle and to the Revolution itself. A short walk takes the visitor into what is left of Yorktown, with a number of the original buildings fully restored, including the home of Augustine Moore, where the terms of surrender were drafted.

Next time I am in my old home town I am going to visit Taft Grade School and see if George Washington's portrait is still hanging in what used to be Miss Ream's sixth-grade classroom. Something tells me it still is. Miss Ream would never have allowed it otherwise.

God Bless You, Mr. Mapes

Gooseberry Falls is an interesting but rather familiar attraction to northland dwellers driving up Lake Superior's shoreline. However for a thirteen-year-old Boy Scout fresh from the corn and soybean flats of Illinois, the sheer power and thunder of the falls was awesome in the early June sunshine.

There were nine of us on the two-week expedition led by Paul Mapes, a middle-aged manual arts teacher in the junior high and a dedicated scoutmaster. We always called him "Mister" Mapes. Although not a tall man, he had a bearing, an authority that commanded respect. Mr. Mapes's specialty was woodworking, and as a careful craftsman, he taught us how to convert pieces of wood into useful kitchen items without running our fingers through the bandsaw. But it was in campcraft that his influence was most appreciated by our noisy, skinny group of adolescents.

He had constructed a wooden trailer that was towed behind his rebuilt six-cylinder Rockne (anyone remember the Rockne?) and transported kids, camp gear, and food on the 1,100-mile round trip. How our destination of Minnesota's Gooseberry State Park

had been selected was never made clear. It took two onerous, strife-filled days of driving to get there, but was worth it. With loud whoops we unloaded the trailer, staked out our tents, and ran through the woods to view the falls. In those days it seemed like we ran wherever we went. Walking was not on our agenda.

As the only real angler in the group, I had studied up on the trout streams of Lake Superior's North Shore. My source was the magazine rack at Doc Lenz's drugstore, where I had furtively, during the winter, thumbed through copies of *Field and Stream, National Sportsman,* and other periodicals, until Doc caught me and threw me out. In 1934, no thirteen-year-old youngster had cash to purchase sports magazines.

Trout streams did not exist where I grew up, but from my reading I came to understand that brook and rainbow trout were in a trophy category somewhat above the catfish and carp inhabiting our turbid Illinois waters. While Mr. Mapes and the other eight members of our expedition clambered over the granite ledges and pursued wildflower-garnished foot paths, I cast into the icy pools between the falls and Lake Superior. My equipment was a battered split bamboo fly rod, simple reel, kinky enameled line, catgut leader, and a Royal Coachman wet fly, the only fly I owned. Wonder of wonders, through dint of persistence and sheer luck, I managed to plant the hook in the jaw of a fifteen-inch speckled warrior that engaged in explosive combat, eventually surrendered, and was hauled triumphantly back to camp where it was admired, photographed, dressed out, and broiled over a bed of coals . . . Scout-style.

It was that experience, more than any other, that drew me back to Minnesota in adulthood, eventually resulting in a migration with my family from the corn flats to the north woods some thirty-five years ago. Quite often, as I pursue trout and other game species in the myriad streams and lakes of the granite shield country, my thoughts drift back to those early days and the wonderful camping trips we were privileged to enjoy through the sacrifice and commitment of our scoutmaster, camping trips in which we were also absorbing some of his characteristics of honesty, courage, patience, and camaraderie.

Our old scoutmaster has long ago been laid to rest beneath the prairie sod, but I think of him often. To him and to all those who have taken time out of their lives to help young people develop a reverence for our magnificent outdoors and consideration for one another, may this heartfelt word of appreciation be offered: God bless you, Mr. Mapes. You made the world a better place.

Doing the
Rabbit Twist

"All we need is twenty feet of barbed wire."

Wally Stettler squinted thoughtfully at the open end of a six-inch clay tile protruding from the dirt slope at the end of a grass-rimmed drainage ditch.

"See those tracks?" he pointed at scuff marks in the ditch. "A rabbit's using that tile as a den . . . if he's in there, we can twist him out."

Twist him? At age fourteen, I naturally deferred to Wally's expertise. A dozen years my senior, he had grown up hunting rabbits on his family's farm and those of our neighbors. In matters involving pursuit of game I had learned not to question, but to observe and listen.

A bitter December wind had scattered a light dusting of snow over woodland and pasture, corn and soybean stubble. Although the snow was too scant for serious tracking, in the sheltered drainage ditch, telltale footprints indicated where our long-eared quarry had recently traveled. It was a week before Christmas, and our intent was to secure a brace or two of plump rabbits for a side dish of hasenpfeffer to accompany the traditional holiday turkey.

Our efforts to the moment had been ruefully slim. Apparently the zero temperatures had driven the rabbits from grain field and grassland coverts to seek shelter in underground burrows, culverts, and drain tiles. Although this tile indicated recent use, I was mystified as to how barbed wire entered the equation. In any event, I trailed Wally as he searched abandoned fence rows, eventually recovering a satisfactory, albeit rusted, strand.

Wally dragged the wire back to the ditch and shoved one end into the tile with a circular, twisting motion.

"When the barbs get tangled in the rabbit's fur," he explained, "all we have to do is pull him out."

It all seemed very improbable, but Wally had demonstrated before a number of hunting and trapping skills not usually found in outdoor publications. "Hah!" he exclaimed at length. "Contact!"

While still twisting, he began pulling the wire back out of the tile, the metal strands now alive with resistance, indicating some unseen force jerking on the other end. "Get ready to shoot when I haul him out," Wally warned. "He may slip loose from the wire and take off running."

I stepped forward, cocked the hammer on my single-shot 20-gauge and tensed for action.

There was a scuffle of claws and a flurry of flying dirt at the mouth of the tile. At the same moment, Wally dropped the wire and dove out of the ditch. "Look out!" he screeched. "It ain't a rabbit!"

Emerging into the daylight, furry tail tangled in the barbed wire, was a very large and furious skunk. We virtually flew upwind, pausing only when a hundred yards of space separated us from our enraged adversary. Eventually, the skunk extracted himself from the wire and stamped back into his lair, but not before he laid an acrid layer of scent over the surrounding landscape.

At length, Wally and I tiptoed back to retrieve the shotguns, abandoned in our headlong retreat. The weapons, as I recall, maintained a pungent aura for more than a week. And Christmas dinner was not graced by side dishes of hasenpfeffer that year.

Hockey at Heiden's Slough

Christmas vacation! Ah, words of joy. A reprieve from the piercing scrutiny of our fourth-grade teacher. A time to think of food, gifts, carols, and laughter . . . and hockey on the frozen surface of Heiden's Slough.

The Heiden farm, like many in our area, was owned and operated by third-generation Germans. Like the others, they milked cows, raised chickens, sold eggs, grew corn, oats, and hay, plowed with horses, and eked out a very meager living. But unlike the other farmers, the Heidens had a slough of forty acres, ten of which composed a cattail-rimmed pond. It was our hockey rink.

Thus it was that two days after Christmas, the six members of our neighborhood gang, the Kerwin Terrace Terrors, met in one of the frequent face-offs with our mortal enemies, the Briargate Bunch. With a hand ax, we determined that the ice was indeed two inches thick, sufficient to sustain our weight, whereupon we erected two poles at each end of the "rink" to delineate the goal cages. Then we put on our skates. That is, we locked them onto the soles of our shoes.

There were perhaps two or three skaters among both teams who owned lace-on shoe skates—modern skates with the shoe and blade as one integral unit. The rest of us had clamp-on blades that were fastened in place on the soles of our shoes by use of a key, which tightened adjustable clamps that gripped the sole of the shoe. These were further reinforced by a leather strap buckled over each ankle.

Hockey sticks were branched tree limbs, cut and trimmed to length. The puck was a Carnation milk can. There were no officials, no penalties. Frequent arguments were settled by arbitration, sometimes vehement.

My immediate concern, however, involved my skates. They kept coming loose. In the bitter cold, my fingers apparently could not turn the skate key tight enough. The problem was solved by the biggest and oldest member of our gang, Gino Moretti, who, at age thirteen, was infinitely stronger. And smarter. He used a spike as a lever to turn the skate key and locked the clamps securely in place.

Indeed, Gino screwed the skates so solidly to my shoes that after the game I continued to practice some elementary figure skating around the slough. Unfortunately, when darkness began to descend and it was time to go home, I discovered that Gino had already gone. And my skate key was in his jacket pocket. I could not get the skates off my shoes. Nor could I walk home in the snow in my stocking feet; so I hobbled home with my skates on, one miserable mile. At home, I took off my shoes and surveyed my blistered, purple, and pained feet. Mother filled a pan with hot water and Epsom salts in which to soak my injured members. My father retrieved the missing skate key and got my skates unclamped from my shoes.

But my hockey career was severely impacted for several weeks until my feet healed. Perhaps it was that episode that eventually switched my sports preference to basketball. Basketball, I found, could be played indoors. And with nothing to clamp on my feet.

A Glorious
Fourth of July

Fourth of July, 1934, dawned dry, hazy, windless, and hot. Cornfields drooped from an extensive drought that choked most of the Midwest.

The nation was in the throes of the Great Depression, a financial disaster that had somehow invaded my own personal finances. The $1.50 weekly salary from my newspaper route had been unwisely spent, so I had no money for fireworks. The financial constraints of the Great Depression had finally encompassed my own personal resources.

By 8:00 A.M. there were numerous pops and bangs up the street where my grade-school peers were busy shooting off firecrackers amidst shouts of joy. Dejected and morose, I slouched in the shade of our front porch.

At that point, my father came outside. "Not celebrating the Fourth?" he inquired.

"Busted," I said. "No money."

In that era no one dared ask their parents for money. You either earned it or did without.

Dad squinted at me sharply, then motioned toward the family Model A. "Hop in . . . let's go see if we can find some fireworks."

My hopes suddenly shot skyward. Perhaps, with luck, I might acquire a package or two of firecrackers. Possibly even some three-inch salutes, which could blow a coffee can five feet into the air. In moments we were driving through the business area, then pulled up to a red, white, and blue fireworks stand and stopped.

"How's it going, Eddie?" Dad asked the proprietor, a sour-faced young man in white pants and white shirt with rolled sleeves.

"Slow," Eddie mumbled, chewing on a toothpick. "Nobody's got any money." Dad priced firecrackers, fountains, and pinwheels, then moved toward the bigger stuff—Roman candles and sky-rockets.

"How much for all this stuff?" Dad asked.

"Prices are on the boxes."

"No . . . I mean the whole works."

Eddie gulped. "You mean everything?"

"Yeah. Everything."

Eddie spit out the toothpick and leaped into action, pencil and pad in hand. "Listen," he confided. "I'll give you a real deal . . . fifteen bucks over what I paid."

He showed dad the figures on his pad. Dad nodded and pulled out his billfold. "Box it all up."

I almost fainted. Never in my life had I seen my father take such an interest in so worthy an enterprise, Fourth of July included. We hauled carton after carton to the Model A, filling the entire back seat to the roof, then piling additional boxes on my lap in front. The two huge final cartons were roped to the Ford, one between the headlights on the front bumper and the other secured to the spare tire bolted on the back of the chassis. We'd bought everything!

When we began unloading in front of the house, my mother came out, stifled a scream, and stood glaring, tears forming in her eyes. Finally she gasped out, "What have you done? You must have spent your whole month's paycheck!"

Indeed, father had. Somewhat lamely he replied, "Well, it's the Fourth of July and the kid ought to have something to celebrate with, for Pete's sake."

Mom let out a screech of despair. "Here I skimp and scrape to save a nickel here and there on the grocery bill and you go blow goodness-know-how-much on firecrackers!" She stamped back inside, slamming the door.

Dad smiled wanly. "Women don't understand these things," he whispered, and winked.

July 4, 1934, went down in the history of our neighborhood as the day my father financed the biggest fireworks display ever seen on the west side of town. Far into the night we shot off Roman candles, skyrockets, pinwheels, and cherry bombs, and even the smallest kids had sparklers to wave.

It took my mother most of the summer to recover her good nature. On numerous occasions she reminded us of "that Fourth of July insanity." But oh, what a glorious day it had been. A day when my father assumed heroic proportions I had never know he possessed. In my adolescent mind he stood tall as Washington, Jefferson, Hamilton, Thomas Paine, Ethan Allen. My father, the patriot.

That Magnificent Car

I had heard it was for sale. It sat on its four thin tires in Clyde Sheridan's backyard, gleaming black enamel and bright chrome trim. The top was canvas, supported buggy-style, with no side curtains.

"Whatcha want for it?"

"Eighteen bucks." Clyde wiggled a toothpick in his mouth.

Admittedly, eighteen dollars was not a lot for an automobile. This one had seen some wear, since it was a Henry Ford 1916 two-seater. The year was 1938.

"Will it run?"

"Runs good. Lemme show you."

Clyde set the spark and gas levers on the steering shaft, went around in front, and spun the hand crank. The car bucked, puffed smoke, and roared into action.

"Climb in."

He got behind the wheel, I slid onto the passenger seat, and we were off, Clyde demonstrating how the gears shifted with foot pedals on the floor.

I wanted that car. But I didn't have eighteen bucks, a rather princely sum during the Depression. "Give you eight down," I said. "The rest two bucks a week."

Clyde shifted the toothpick in his mouth. Squinted. "OK. You miss a payment, it's mine back."

"Yeah."

He wrote out a bill of sale, and I handed over eight bucks and drove away. I owned a car! A real car! A high school junior, and I had my own car!

Had to impress somebody. On the hilly east side of town was this classy young lady from high school. Marge. Pulled up by her front door. I didn't get out, afraid to shut off the engine. Instead, I honked the horn. Ooh-gah!

"Somebody out in front, Marge," I heard her mother yell. "If he was a gentleman, he would park the car and come knock on the door." Marge came bouncing out of the house, circled my car, shook her head, and slid onto the seat. "Where'll we go?"

"Downtown and back."

I let out the clutch and away we went, through the middle of downtown, where my vintage vehicle drew a number of stares amid all the 1938s, '37s, and other recent models. Then back up Maple Avenue to Marge's house, where I dropped her off.

"Wanna go to the football game Saturday?"

"In this?" She thought a minute. "Why not?"

My heart was hammering. Somewhere I knew I had to acquire the money for the game plus the two-dollar car payment for next week. I drove into the alley back of our house, shut off the ignition, and got out. My father was standing by the garage. How did he know I had just bought a car?

"What's that?" He pointed a finger at the Ford.

"My new car."

"Uh huh. How much?"

"Uh . . . eighteen bucks."

He nodded. "Have to get insurance."

"What?"

"Can't drive without insurance. You're a minor and I am liable for whatever you do."

Insurance, I discovered, was going to cost more than the car. And I still owed Clyde ten dollars. The financial burden was overwhelming. Sadly, I flipped the crank and drove the Ford back to Clyde's house.

"You're back." Clyde said, the toothpick bouncing up an down.

"Can't keep the car." I said. "You didn't tell me about insurance. You've got to take it back."

The toothpick twitched faster. "I got to make something on this deal. I'll give you four bucks back."

Recognizing defeat, I regretfully took the four, patted the chromed radiator sadly, and headed for home on foot. At least with the four dollars my pocket I could take Marge to the Saturday game if dad let me use his 1936 V-8.

That was fifty-nine years go. Title to a number of cars have come and gone since. But the 1916 Ford stands out even though I owned it for only one afternoon. First car. It was a beauty. Oh, yeah. Marge dumped me for a senior with a 1928 Model A.

An Electrifying
Camp Experience

The first warm Friday afternoon of May, Art, Don, and I raced home from high school, gathered up our camping outfits, and had Don's mother drive us to the DuPage River. In 1939, few farmers cared who wandered through their fields and woodlands; thus we could follow the watercourse downstream for eight to ten miles over the weekend and have another of our parents pick us up Sunday night at the little village of Shorewood. Friday-to-Sunday campouts were a regular occurrence, and this one began auspiciously.

Hiking through emerging timothy and sweet clover, we savored the sounds of cows being called for milking, the raucous cries of distant, homeward-bound crows, the staccato chorus of spring frogs, the delicious sense of freedom from the unbearable confinement of school.

Our camp that night was on a river bend, in the shelter of a willow thicket where we tied out the corners of the tattered square of canvas that served as our tent. Sleeping bags, foam mats, and other paraphernalia were not yet invented. We pitched our blankets on the ground and accommodated our bodies to the roots and rocks. Up to about midnight.

A clap of thunder ushered in a horrendous rainstorm that bent the willows and swished through our shelter. Art had the only flashlight, and under its pale yellow beam we sought dry islands beneath the canvas while fighting hordes of ravaging mosquitoes. When the sun rose at dawn we each silently offered thanks to whatever Higher Power intervened that our lives had been spared.

Unable to find dry wood for a breakfast fire, we stuffed down a few graham crackers, rolled up our soggy blankets, shouldered our knapsacks, and prepared to trek off downstream. As we crossed from one farm to the next, we encountered a taut three-strand barbed-wire fence. And while we argued about whether to go over or under this obstacle, none of us noticed that the middle strand was secured to each steel fence post by a porcelain insulator. This rather recent innovation in farm country was an electric wire, which was aimed at discouraging cows from running against and knocking over fences.

It was long-legged Don who finally took matters in hand. With one movement he threw his pack over the fence, grabbed the top wire, shoved his left leg through, straddled the middle wire, and grabbed it with his hand. The moment he touched the middle wire, he received a jolt, then another, and another. From the all-night rain the wet grass considerably magnified the charge.

"Whuh! Whuh! Whuh! . . . Whoo! Whoo Whoo! . . . Ow! Ow! WOW!" Don screamed, his body twitching as he rocked between the top two wires.

Art doubled up and fell to the ground laughing, but I was terrified that Don was being electrocuted before our eyes. Luckily, when the fence had been erected, an extra steel post had been left leaning against a nearby tree. I grabbed the post and flipped it over the center wire, effectively shorting it out. Ashen faced, Don struggled to get free. "I coulda got killed!" he screeched through shaky lips.

Art laughed even harder, nearly precipitating a fistfight. Eventually we got our knapsacks and bodies through the fence and continued downstream, eyes alert to any further porcelain insulators. The following evening, Art's dad picked us up at Shorewood in his Packard.

"Anything happen on the camping trip?"

"Nope. Nothin' happened."

We never told our parents about the electric fence . . . or anything else. We were always afraid they wouldn't let us go again.

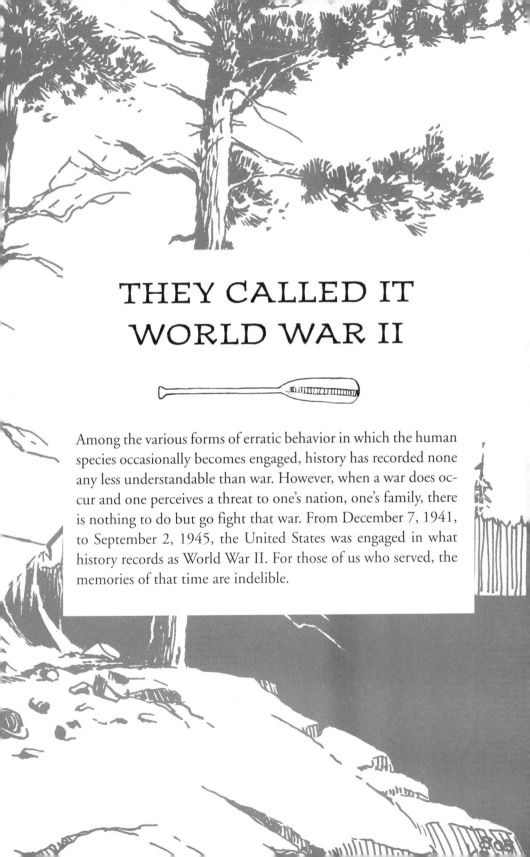

THEY CALLED IT WORLD WAR II

Among the various forms of erratic behavior in which the human species occasionally becomes engaged, history has recorded none any less understandable than war. However, when a war does occur and one perceives a threat to one's nation, one's family, there is nothing to do but go fight that war. From December 7, 1941, to September 2, 1945, the United States was engaged in what history records as World War II. For those of us who served, the memories of that time are indelible.

John Clemente and Benito Mussolini

"Mussolini is-a greatest-a man in-a history of-a Italy!"

Mr. Clemente loved to hold forth over the counter in his little neighborhood grocery store, ticking off on his fingers the reported accomplishments of the new Italian dictator.

"He's-a build-a new roads, and-a new schools, and the trains-a all runna on time! Everybody he's-a gotta job under Mussolini!"

I heard this quite often since Clemente's store was on my paper route and he would laud his hero even to a twelve-year-old kid dropping off the evening edition of the *Herald-News*. In the middle of the Great Depression, times were tough. Many people, like the Clementes, were desperately trying to pay their bills and raise their families.

John worked long hours, not only in his store but in a large garden out back where he raised produce to sell. His wife, also an immigrant from Europe, was a very quiet, pleasant woman who managed to feed and clothe two well-behaved daughters and send them to our neighborhood public school.

The adult Clementes had left Italy sometime after John's service in World War I and had come to the Land of Promise to make a new life. The new life was hard. They scrimped, saved, bought the small store, only to scrimp and save some more. In our town, unemployment was running over 25 percent. Temporary employment was in low-paying government projects like the WPA.

On the other hand, news from the "Old Country" began sounding more and more appealing. Hitler had raised Germany to a mighty economic and military power. His fascist ally, Benito Mussolini, had taken over a foundering Italy, bent on raising it to former Roman grandeur. Indeed, the Italian government magazines and newspapers sent to John described in vivid detail how Italy was on its way to greatness. John began savings nickels and dimes, eventually acquiring enough for an economy-class trip "back home." He could talk about nothing else for weeks before his pilgrimage. He was going back to the scene of his childhood, to visit his uncles, aunts, cousins, nephews, nieces. To view first hand the rising glory of the new Roman Empire.

One evening, a few weeks after John had left, as I was dropping off the newspaper, I found a very grim-faced, tearful Mrs. Clemente. "John is in jail in Italy," she groaned.

"What?" Even at age twelve, I was aware through watching movies that jails were forbidding institutions.

According to Mrs. Clemente's choked testimony, John found things in Italy were not exactly as advertised. Outspoken as usual, he was quickly arrested for exercising free speech, something not allowed under the fascist regime. There followed considerable excitement in our neighborhood as Mrs. Clemente pleaded, scrounged, and borrowed enough money to pay John's fine and get the Italian government to release him.

Then, one evening, a somewhat subdued Mr. Clemente appeared back behind the counter at his small store.

"How were things in Italy?" I asked, as I handed him the *Herald-News.*

"Not-a good. " John muttered. "That Mussolini! He's-a bum . . . a-nothin' but a bum!"

After that the subject of John's trip was never discussed. But I noticed that on the Fourth of July, a large American flag flew proudly from a wooden staff in front of the grocery store.

Thanksgiving Feast

November 24, 1943, dawned with a few wisps of smoke rising from the jumbled wreckage and shredded trees on an island named Betio. From the relative calm of adjacent Bairiki, hundreds of Marines lay in the shade of swaying palms, staring at that strip of coral and sand two and a quarter miles long by a half mile wide, which had been a horrifying hellhole for the past seventy-six hours.

Betio was the heavily fortified command post on a curving, island-dotted atoll the world would know as Tarawa. In those seventy-six hours, 3,301 Marines had fallen to concentrated, point-blank gunfire from a network of concrete bunkers. And 4,690 Japanese, entrenched in those bunkers, had been killed by rifles, machine guns, hand grenades, and flame throwers.

But now the guns were silent. The wounded had been moved to white hospital ships in the bay. The atoll lagoon lay pale blue, barely ruffled by a light ocean breeze. Those of us who were survivors, by some uncomprehending hand of fate, stared at the tropical serenity with eyes that had seen too much.

And then, from out on the lagoon, came a shout: "Fish!"

One by one, Marines lurched to their feet squinting at two figures stumbling ashore holding huge, silvery mackerel by their

forked tails. The war forgotten, dozens of battle-scared veterans dropped their rifles and crashed into the water.

The significance of this should be explained: It was Thanksgiving Day, and our digestive tracts were totally at odds with the dry and dreary K rations consumed in foxholes the past three days. Thanksgiving dinner, we were informed, would be more of the same. But out there in the lagoon lay a feast.

With the tide out, we observed a formation of low stone walls—fish traps built prewar in the shallows by native islanders. The walls were erected in the shape of a heart, perhaps a hundred feet across. When the tide was in, fish swarmed into the lagoon, bumped into the walls, and followed them to a notch at the very top of the heart, where several stones had been removed. The fish then poured through this gap, only to be trapped within the walls when the tide went out.

In short order, over a hundred Marines were wading among the thrashing schools of mackerel, grabbing for the curved tails. It took only minutes to secure a brace, and with a flopping six-pound fish in each hand, we waded back to shore.

Moments later we had the fish dressed out and fires kindled from dead, dry coconut logs. Soon we were tending dozens of mackerel broiling over hot coals, while other Marines shinnied up nearby trees to knock down a host of "green" coconuts. The tops were lopped off with machetes, revealing the sweet milk inside (we knew from experience in the tropics that "ripe" coconuts, while edible, were apt to cause digestive problems known as "the G.I. drizzlies."

A brief letter I sent home to my mother read: "Dear Mom: Am O.K. no matter what you read in the papers. Thanksgiving feast today consisted of broiled mackerel and coconut milk eaten in the shade of towering palm trees on a scenic south sea island. I would rather have your turkey and trimmings at home."

There was strict military censorship, and none of us made any attempt to describe the bitter battle that had cost so many lives. We left that for the war correspondents and newsreel cameras. It was enough that our families heard from us. And our hearts went out to those parents who we knew would receive the War Department notices: "We regret to inform you . . ."

Later, the battalion chaplain, Father Michaels, held a brief prayer service under the trees. Everyone attended—Catholic, Protestant, and Jew—helmets off, heads bowed. Already the SeaBee units were laying out the cemetery and erecting row upon row of white crosses where hundreds of our comrades would rest forever beneath the glistening coral.

We watched the sun dip into the western sea, well aware that while we had punched a significant wedge into Japan's Pacific defenses, there would be thousands more white crosses erected on dozens of not-yet-known islands before this war would be over. Most of all, each of us gave silent thanks that we had been spared . . . to go on and fight another day.

Thanksgiving, 1943. Not many of us are left now, but those of us who are will never forget it.

A Very Personal War

We are much older now. What hair we have left is mostly white. Some of us walk with difficulty. But fifty years ago we were young, brash, vigorous, and proud. The combat troops of World War II.

Last month the nation commemorated VE Day, Victory in Europe. The surrender of German forces on May 8, 1945. In August we will commemorate the surrender of Japanese armed forces, August 14, 1945. Only it started a year before that. It started on June 15, 1944, with the invasion of the islands of Saipan and Tinian. It would be from the airfield on Tinian that four-engine B-29s would fly to bomb the Japanese homeland. From there the *Enola Gay* would fly with the nuclear weapon that brought four years of bloodshed to an abrupt stop.

However, those of us on that June 15, 1944, invasion did not recognize the grand strategy. Our personal war lay on the beach just off the starboard side of the troop transport, one of some six-hundred ships in Task Force 58 at Saipan. Big guns on the battleships and cruisers pounded the island. Dive bombers from carriers screamed in overhead.

For those of us preparing to enter that inferno in tracked steel landing craft, it was one more familiar prelude to the same costly, blood-spattered hells of Guadalcanal, Tarawa, Kwajalein, and Eniwetok. We were what the military liked to term "seasoned troops." Perhaps "survivors" is more apt. We had learned the trade of war. We were adept at delivering destruction and death with swift efficiency.

We watched the bombardment of the shore and the capital city of Garapan, hoping it would make our landing less costly. But our intuition was that a clever, dedicated enemy would have taken cover back from the beach and would engage the first wave to hit the shore. Combat wise, we were seldom wrong.

We were well aware that we would be entering a familiar hell of crashing shells, yammering machine guns, a hell of mud, blood, screams of wounded and dying. But we didn't know one more horrifying element would be added: the Marianas were the first islands we would hit where there was a large population of civilians—twenty thousand in Garapan alone. It would be the first time we witnessed the sickening toll on terrified women, children, and the very old, noncombatants caught in the crossfire of war. Though battle-wise and hardened, we were not prepared for what we saw.

We tried as best we could to sort them out, to segregate and shield the civilians. Our Navy corpsmen, our doctors and nurses, already working day and night to patch torn bodies of our troops, administered to the civilians as they were brought in, too.

Of course we had no way of knowing all this was about to happen as we watched from the ship's deck. The time was 0700 hours—7 A.M. by civilian clocks. Corporal Larry Zink and I squinted at the fury of shellfire and bombs hurling a two-hundred-foot wall of dirt, smoke, and fire into the air.

"You know what June 15 is back home in Illinois?" I asked softly.

Larry never took his eyes from the bombardment. "No. What day is it?"

"June 15 is opening day in the 1944 bass season," I answered. "I wish I was watching dawn on the Fox River."

Larry managed a faint grin. "I wish I was fishing with you on the Fox River, Sarge."

We buckled the chin straps on our helmets, climbed down the ladder into the landing craft. June 15, 1944. There will probably be little or no mention of Saipan and Tinian among the speeches given this summer commemorating VJ Day. But there will be some mention, perhaps criticism, about the nuclear bomb that flew from Tinian on the *Enola Gay*, fifty-five years ago, abruptly ending a bitter war.

For those of us who were on the islands in 1944, the memory can never be erased. At least not until that time we join the comrades we placed beneath the white crosses on those palm-shaded shores.

Armistice Day

November 11 is Veterans Day.

Words and numbers officially on the calendar.

There will be some sound bites on TV, required comments by members of the Congress and the President, and quiet dinners in American Legion and Veterans of Foreign Wars club rooms across the nation. But for those of us old enough to remember, November 11 will always be "Armistice Day," a day set aside not only by this nation but by a war-weary world to commemorate the end in 1918 of what was then the most terrible conflict in world history.

As grade-schoolers, we were well aware of the history involving World War I. We had read about the assassination of Archduke Francis Ferdinand of Austria by a Serbian nationalist—the spark that ignited the conflict involving Germany, France, England, Austria, Italy, Russia, Japan, Turkey, Belgium, the Netherlands, and Greece. We knew that leading up to the conflict there had been endless posturing, threats, and counterthreats by world politicians and military figures, all spoiling for a fight. And how they lacked comprehension of the horrors that machine guns, tanks, massed artillery, aerial warfare, and poison gas would inflict upon millions of troops and civilians alike. We knew the

United States entered the war in 1917 as England and France were near collapse and that 1,200,000 Yanks in the trenches were a decisive factor in Germany's defeat, with the Armistice taking effect at 11 A.M., November 11, 1918.

In the years immediately following that war, Armistice Day was a major holiday, celebrated with newspaper and magazine articles, speeches, and parades. Everybody in my hometown went downtown in the morning to watch the parade. Sidewalks were jammed. The elders had tears in their eyes, but we kids were enthralled by the blaring bands, the pageantry, the sound as hundreds of marching feet thudded on the pavement in unison. Little did we know that in a few short years many of us would be in uniform and on our way to combat in World War II.

Oh, but those early Armistice Days were glorious to us kids. First came the American Legion and Veterans of Foreign Wars color guards, followed by the Legion band, ranks of uniformed nurses who served, and a dozen cars loaded with Gold Star mothers, mothers of sons lost in the war. Endless rows of uniformed veterans marched past, the men who had stopped the kaiser's legions in places named Belleau Wood, Argonne, Château Thierry, and St. Mihiel. Proud men who marched erect in perfect step, barring a limp here and there, eyes straight ahead, flags flying. There were high school bands, and then the thin, graying ranks of Spanish American War veterans.

At ten minutes before eleven, whistles blew, and the marching feet abruptly halted, the bands fell silent. Everyone—veterans and bystanders alike—faced toward the east in silence. Precisely at eleven, a bugle softly sounded taps for those who did not return from France. Then there was the crash of cymbals, the bands struck up a lively Sousa march, the crowd roared, and the parade went on.

Somewhere in the midst of all the marching figures appeared an open touring car decorated with red, white, and blue bunting.

Riding alone in the back seat was a frail-looking, white-haired man in a faded blue uniform. The crowd grew respectfully silent as the touring car moved slowly past.

"Commander Cunningham," someone whispered. "The last living veteran of the Civil War."

We youngsters stared in disbelief. How could this pale-eyed wraith have fought in Lincoln's war? How could he have fought anyone? How little we understood about age.

Again this year, the graying seniors who served in World War II will quietly meet for dinner in veterans' club rooms across America. Those very few living survivors of the first World War can no longer meet with us, but they will be remembered. While the nation celebrates Veterans Day, those of us from World War II will always honor November 11 as Armistice Day, a salute to those men and women who served their country in 1917 and 1918 and who saw to it that veterans who returned in 1945 had the G.I. Bill of Rights, including free education and medical and employment benefits. They did not forget us. We will not forget them.

Dad's Victory Garden

"Your father has the finest Victory Garden in the entire neighborhood." So read the letter from my mother in 1942 as I sat in the shade of a huge banyan tree growing on the bullet-shredded island of Guadalcanal. I was part of a contingent of U.S. Marines engaged in the first attempt to dismantle the Japanese "Greater Asian Co-Prosperity Sphere," which encompassed much of the South Pacific at the time.

This garden news was rendered somewhat unbelievable because my father, although a skilled engineer, had never to my knowledge so much as raised a radish. It was over two years and three more amphibious assaults later that I was furloughed home and had the opportunity to view this agricultural marvel first-hand. Victory gardens, it should be noted, were a home-front wartime promotion of President Franklin Delano Roosevelt, an enterprise designed to supplement the nation's food supply and free up crops for shipment to our overseas allies.

Prior to the war, it had been my father's custom, after supper, to head for the living room, sink into his favorite chair, and absorb the evening newspaper. However, the first evening I was home, he pushed back from the dining room table, headed for the back door, armed himself with hoe and rake, ånd strode to the garden plot, where he labored until nearly dark. Laid out with mathematical precision in a 50 x 100 foot rectangle of rich, black Midwest loam, my father's garden had been carefully ploughed, planted, fertilized, cultivated, and watered to produce a bounteous harvest. There grew a bumper crop of peas, beans, lettuce, spinach, radishes, cucumbers, squash, peppers, muskmelons, onions, and sweet corn. Indeed, father's garden appeared head and shoulders above those of the neighbors.

"Gee, Pop," I said in wonderment. "I didn't know you could make a garden like this."

"If you grew up in the late 1800s in a large family, you were expected to work in the family garden," Dad replied. With three brothers and eight sisters, he explained, it was necessary to raise much of their food, which was not only consumed as ripened, but also dried, canned, or stored in root cellars for the winter.

When my two-week furlough was up, I returned to active duty with a new appreciation for my father and a warm feeling that he was contributing not only his engineering ability toward the war effort, but also his gardening skills. I looked forward to the end of the war, praying that if I survived, I could return and work side by side with dad, growing food in our family garden.

On September 2, 1945, the Japanese signed papers of surrender on board the USS *Missouri,* and a few weeks later, along with a horde of lucky and thankful ex-servicemen, I headed for home. My arrival coincided with suppertime, and following an excellent meal of roast beef, mashed potatoes, and gravy, I announced that I was ready to go forth and help dad in the garden.

"Not necessary," he said, heading for the living room and his favorite chair.

As he buried himself with a sigh in the upholstery and unfolded the newspaper, I inquired, "What about the garden, Pop? What about the weeds?"

Dad glanced for a moment over the top of the newspaper. "The war," he said with finality, "is over."

And I guess it really was. And so was the victory garden.

Winton's Winged Warrior of WW II

November 11, 1998.

Armistice Day for the nearly vanished veterans of World War I. Veteran's Day for the rapidly thinning ranks of World War II servicemen. When the bugle sounds for our departed comrades this November 11, those of us who can will stand erect and once more salute the flag we fought for. And none will stand taller or straighter than eighty-one-year-old Tauno Maki of Winton, Minnesota. This is his story.

It was a calm, sunshiny day, November 10, 1944, a blue sky dotted with white cumulus. Twelve Flying Fortresses composing Squadron 511 took off from Northhamptonshire, England, each with eight thousand pounds of bombs aimed for a target at Ruhland, Germany, just north of Berlin.

At the controls of Fortress No. 4-6139 were First Pilot Lt. Donald Hadley and copilot Lt. Tauno Maki. It was the crew's second mission, although the plane had flown thirty other missions with a different crew. The four 1,200 horsepower Curtiss Wright engines droned steadily as the English Channel and North

Sea passed below. The squadron skirted the North Frisian Islands, cut across the Kiel peninsula, and zeroed in on the target. The calm was suddenly shattered.

"All hell broke loose," says Maki. Like a horde of mosquitos, dozens of Messerschmitt 109s and Focke-Wulf 190s swarmed over the bombers. Twelve .50 caliber machine guns on each Flying Fort were spewing out thousands of tracers. Escorting U.S. P-51s and P-47s bore in, engaging the Germans in a monumental melee of fire and explosions.

"Planes were going down in flames, and airmen were bailing out in chutes," Maki recalls. "In minutes, six of the twelve Fortresses in the squadron were hit and going down; eleven airmen were killed outright, forty-three taken prisoner."

Maki's ship took 20 mm hits on No. 3 and No. 4 engines, and plummeted toward earth. The two pilots managed to gain control and leveled off, flying on the remaining two engines. Unfortunately, the fuel transfer mechanism was also hit, and the crippled plane was rapidly running out of fuel.

"It was a wild ride," recalls Maki. "Downhill all the way across Germany, extremely low over the Meuse River where General George Patton's 3rd Army was rocking the Nazi forces back on their heels. We came in extremely low over the city of Metz, spotted an open farm field on our left, banked 180 degrees, and prepared for a belly landing. At the same time Al, our tail gunner, was screaming, 'I got that S.O.B.! I got that S.O.B.!' He was credited with shooting down an FW 190 and wanted the world to know it."

The plane slammed into a beet field, plowed a furrow straight toward an ancient stone château, but shuddered to a stop a hundred meters short. As the crew scrambled out, thankful to be alive, one crewman congratulated the pilots: "That was the smoothest landing you guys ever made."

When the dust settled, townsfolk from nearby Villiers Lez Hoest told them they were in Belgium and had landed at an opportune moment. One week earlier, the village had been in Nazi hands and the château was the site where several members of the Resistance were captured and executed by the retreating Germans.

Fortunately, they were within 3rd Army lines. The crew was taken to Brussels and thence back to England, was given another plane, and flew thirty-three more missions before war's end. But the story does not end there.

Fifty years later, to the day, the residents of Villiers Lez Hoest paid airfare and expenses for the four remaining members of Flying Fortress 4-6139 to attend a reunion, where the airmen were honored by a grateful Belgian populace who never forgot the gallantry and sacrifice of American servicemen who liberated that nation from the grip of Adolph Hitler.

Spare, gray-haired, but ramrod straight, sometimes ex-Lt. Tauno Maki walks the streets of his hometown. Occasionally his eyes scan the skies as if watching for his old squadron. "Those Belgians," he says with a note of pride in his voice, "they never forgot . . . never forgot."

TYPEWRITER NORTH

Three years following World War II, after completing some years of higher education in the fields of journalism and illustration and getting married, I was hired by a genial newspaperman, John F. Lux, publisher of the *Joliet (Illinois) Herald-News.* My title was Outdoor Writer, and as such I was expected to discover and relate to our readers whatever was worthwhile concerning fishing, hunting, camping, trapping, boating, and associated activities, plus some coverage of a relatively new public concern over natural resources called "conservation." I had been fortunate enough to grow up in a rural area with a father who introduced me to the outdoor world and with farmland neighbors who taught me the relationship of earth, sun, water, seeds, and hard work. From the *Herald-News,* I moved to the position of Outdoor Editor of the *Chicago Daily News,* from whence I was free to roam much of North America, from the Gulf of Mexico to the edge of the Arctic, and be paid to write about it. Eventually, my travels took me to Ely, Minnesota, and to the wild and fascinating area called the Boundary Waters, with a sparse population of incredibly hardy folk living on its rim.

It was to Ely that my family and I eventually migrated, and there we opened a canoe outfitting business and I began writing for the *Ely Echo.* It is also here in the forest, twenty-two miles from Ely, that my first wife, Lillian, is buried, and that I intend to live out my days with my present wife, Edith, writing and illustrating as God gives me time and strength.

Dancing Spirits
in the Mists

It seems almost sacrilege to stir the colors with a paddle. Chrome yellow, cadmium orange, alizarin crimson, raw sienna, magenta, rose madder, yellow ochre, burnt sienna, cobalt, cerulean blue— a shimmering palette reflecting the shoreline hues and arching sky that glides past the canoe hull in the awesome splendor of a breathtaking October day.

For many of us who live on the rim of the canoe country, or even come a great distance to visit, autumn ushers in a time of magic. Summer's throngs of vacationers are largely gone. Lakes are calm, deserted. Portage trails, damp and pungent, lie carpeted with golden aspen and birch leaves. Loons with drab fall plumage have gathered in nervous flocks, testing wings, muttering low moans, urging their leaders to get the annual migration under-way. Wedges of smaller waterfowl—mallards, wood ducks, black ducks, teal, goldeneye, scaup, widgeon, mergansers—whip on rushing wings across acres of barren stalks recently laden with wild rice.

Beyond the marsh, the forest rim stretches in a muted land-scape of dogwood, willow, and alder shading into the dark gray-ish green of fir, spruce, and pine. High above on cupped pinions, the dark brown offspring of an eagle pair soars the heavens, intent on testing his hunting skills.

It's magic.

At a place where the lake channels narrow between granite shorelines, where a light current carves lazy swirls in the kaleido-scope of reflected color, progress is slowed, fishing rods unlim-bered, lines dropped into the depths. A long pause, a faint tug, an unseen presence pulling downward followed by a sharp hookset, rod tip arching against a line snapped taught. Gyrating upward, pulsing against the rod's relentless pressure, a swirl of gold and black reveals the glistening form of a sleek walleye. One is fol-lowed by a second, and with both secure on the stringer, the rods are laid down, the paddles are picked up. The gods of fishing fortune have provided two walleyes, four fillets, quite ample for supper.

It's magic.

One majestic shoreline aspen appears out of place, trunk slanted horizontal to the ground. White wood chips circling the severed butt reveal the work of a beaver. A third of the foliage lies sub-merged in the lake, and from the limbs concentric ripples indi-cate a live presence.

As the canoe glides silently closer, the hunched-over form of the beaver appears, one beady eye on the canoe while methodi-cally rotating and gnawing bark from a green limb. Finally alarmed at the approaching craft, the beaver stops chewing, tenses, then dives, walloping the lake surface with his broad tail in a thunder-ing splash.

Magic.

As the afternoon wanes, the reflecting shoreline colors lose their intensity as the western sky turns from blue to lavender and yellow. Spruce treetops, like sharp black spires, jut into the brilliant sunset. Almost as though the warmth of the day has been punctured, the temperature is dropping fast, creating streamers of mist that begin to drift across the surface. For the people of the Ojibwe First Nation, the drifting streamers are spirits of long-departed warriors. And who can prove otherwise?

As our paddles drive our craft homeward, we offer silent thanks to those native woodland folk who centuries ago revealed to our ancestors the lore of paddle and canoe, the fascination of becoming one with water, forest, and sky. There is no other word for it:

Magic.

It All Begins
with Bobber

"Whatcha doin', Grampa?"

"Fixing your line with a bobber."

"What's the bobber for?"

"Tells you when you've got a bite."

"How can it tell you?"

"You'll see.'"

After properly impaling a wriggling worm, I dropped the line off the edge of the dock, and the red and white bobber came to rest on the surface of the lake. My three-year-old granddaughter, Jessica, sat alongside me on the sun-drenched, weathered dock boards, her feet dangling into space.

"Ooh!" Jessica let out a gasp as the bobber bounced up and down, then dove. With a slight assist from Grandpa, her fish pole was jerked upward. We could feel a satisfactory tug on the other end.

Jess let out several more "oohs," leaned back against the unseen force on the line below, and, with another slight assist from Grandpa, derricked a gleaming sunfish onto the dock.

Another "Ooh!" She abruptly dropped the fish pole, bent over, and poked the flopping prize with her forefinger. "It's got eyes," she announced.

"Sure has." Grandpa reached across and removed the hook from the fish. "Now pick it up gently and drop it back into the lake."

"Why, Grampa?" A note of dismay crept into her voice.

"Because it's just a little one. If we get some bigger ones, we'll take them up to the cabin and Grandma will cook them for supper."

"Okay." With a plop the fish went back.

That was my granddaughter's first fishing experience, but not her last. We have been fishing at least once every summer since, even now when she is attending college in Oregon.

Like many other grandparents and grandchildren since the invention of the fishhook, my granddaughter and I have found fishing to be an enjoyable, low-key means of linking what sociologists like to call "the generation gap." Fishing is something we can do together, offering up a baited hook to whatever mysteries lurk below, trusting entirely to chance that some finned denizen will wind up on the line.

Fishing also opens up other opportunities.

Together we have inspected a beaver's housing development and, stretched out on a smooth rock shelf, watched sleek herring gulls circle overhead on translucent pinions. We have hiked back into the woods to photograph wildflowers and listened to the tremolo of a solitary loon wending homeward at sunset. On some days we have gathered armloads of dry branches, kindled fires, roasted hot dogs for lunch at lakeside, and just sat and talked.

Perhaps such forays link us in some small way with grandparents of our distant tribal past, who traditionally were charged with teaching grandchildren the legends, family histories, truths, and rules needed to make their way through life. Family ties

were necessarily knit close, a requirement for survival in that ancient time. Perhaps the need still exists.

When the Minnesota fishing season gets underway next year, thousands of grandparents and grandchildren will ply the state's 5,493 lakes and 15,000 miles of streams that contain fish.

Equipment need not be sophisticated. For youngsters, a simple cane pole, line, hook, sinker, bobber, and a can of worms may suffice. Residents age sixty-five or over can acquire a full-season fishing license for a modest $4.50.

As an introduction to the sport, the Department of Natural Resources provides a "Take a Kid Fishing" weekend in mid-June, when adults accompanying youngsters under sixteen can fish free.

Sometimes I picture a distant day when Jess is rigging up a fish pole for grandchildren of her own and a small voice inquires, "Whatcha doin', Grandma?"

And perhaps Jess will smile and answer, "That's exactly the same question I asked your great-great-grandfather many, many years ago."

USFS Gets Even

Maybe it was payback time. Some readers of our newspaper have remarked that I have been just a smidgen critical of the Forest Service. There are some who say even unfair. Anyhow, Kawishiwi District Ranger Art Wirtz invited me to fly over the Little Gabbro fire a week ago, an enterprise that was certainly worth a story. One definitely showing the USFS in a positive light. The controlled natural burn at Ely eventually became big stuff in the metro press last week, but we were there first. Flying over the fire with Wirtz, forester Ralph Bonde, and pilot Wayne Erickson was interesting and educational. We circled around, took some photos, and went back to the seaplane base in Ely. Which is where this particular episode terminated.

They have a new kind of seat belt in the USFS planes these days. In addition to the regular seat belt that buckles across your lap, there are two more straps, one over each shoulder, that clip onto the lap belt. This is so you can't pitch forward and bust your face on the control panel if the plane noses down, heaven forbid. They keep your shoulders in place.

When we got to the seaplane base and unbuckled our belts, I apparently didn't get the belts tucked clear back, out of the way,

and as I was sliding out of the right front seat of the Beaver, one of the hooks on the belt grabbed the seat of my pants. Thin summer pants. Probably made in Bangladesh. In any event, as I slid down to the right pontoon, the seat ripped right out of them. I mean a real, first-class rip. The whole rear end.

I walked off the seaplane dock behind the Forest Service people, so they probably were not aware that my pants were ripped. When I got back to the *Echo,* I inspected the damage, which was pretty extensive. And hilarious to the staff.

So, in a way, maybe the Forest Service got even for some of those critical stories in the past. Only they didn't know it until now. And maybe never would have except it was too doggone funny a story to keep hidden.

For Shame

One of our regular readers sent in an article from the *Wall Street Journal* about England's $75,000 Normark Fishing Contest. The sponsors insist on entrants taking a lie detector test. This has British anglers upset. However, the sponsors note that in 1992 the British Angling Times banned a John Watson from the British Pike Championship when it was reported that he entered the same fish on three separate times in the Fish of the Week category.

"We never have such a problem," the Bass Anglers Sportsman's Society of the U.S. notes. The B.A.S.S. group holds sixteen tournaments with $4 million in prizes in America.

It uses a lie detector all the time.

The Approach
of Springtime

Pea Soup Lake is open.

This may not mean much to most readers, particularly those from out of town, but Pea Soup Lake on the Fernberg Road is one of spring's surest signs of arrival. It is small, shallow, contains nothing much except minnows, but when the ice goes off, it is one more indication that summer is inevitably on the way.

Certainly robins are in yards gathering straw for their nests, ducks are obvious on Shagawa and Burntside Rivers, bird-watchers are toting up sightings of rare arrivals heading northward, and pileated woodpeckers are whomping out chunks of aged popple to enlarge tree-hole dwellings.

In addition, there is the hum of chain saws as two-legged forest dwellers buck up next winter's fuel supply. It took several years for me to understand that early spring is the time to put up wood. There are no bugs in the forest, the underbrush is no factor, and it is easy to move the wood, to the shed, where it can be split and stacked. In addition, the days are cool, which makes work pleasant. Well, as pleasant as splitting and stacking can be.

Most important, the fishing season is not yet open. For some reason, all manner of yard and house work gets very difficult to accomplish once fishing starts. Dedicated anglers feel that fishing is not one of the more important things in life, it is the only thing.

My father initiated me into the sport of angling when I was age three. By the time I was twelve, he had generously assigned to me all of the fish-cleaning chores. In his unique way, he made it clear that if I wanted to go fishing with him, I had to fillet the catch. My father believed in cooperation involving family effort. He gave the orders, I cooperated.

He was, however, a skilled angler and an expert bait-caster. He could toss a lure into shoreline pockets and under overhanging trees with unerring accuracy. I found it difficult to emulate his skill, partly because my reel was an old hand-me-down that seldom worked.

However, I did become somewhat proficient in the use of live bait. There was one trip to Hayward, Wisconsin, in those early days, when my friend Spang and I, using nightcrawlers and fishing from an old rowboat, one morning greatly outfished our fathers. Our stringer of walleyes and bass was wondrous to behold, while they had one fish between them.

Following lunch in the lodge, we went forth again in the afternoon, Spang and me in the rowboat, my father and his pal roaring away in an outboard-powered craft. It took only minutes for Spang and me to discover that we no longer had our bait box in the boat. Where it went was revealed at supper time, when our two fathers returned with an impressive stringer of fish, all caught on nightcrawlers.

Two lessons were clear: 1. Having the right bait is critical if one is to enjoy success. 2. Never trust anyone when it comes to fishing, not even your own dad.

In any event, the chain saw is buzzing. The woodpile is growing satisfactorily. It is now only three weeks until opening of the 1995 walleye season, and the world is daily becoming a finer place in which to live.

John Smrekar, a historian of some note, reminded me of the walleye season in 1966, when the Governor's Opening was held at Ely. Guest of honor was Iowa Governor Harold Hughes, who got delayed because of bad weather and arrived in the evening of opening day. Minnesota Governor Karl Rolvaag, fishing with Smrekar and some other local experts, had taken an incredible stringer of enormous walleyes at Pipestone Falls that day, and Hughes was frantic to get at the fish. In the morning, anglers were loading up at Waters's dock on Fall Lake, Rolvaag was in his boat, and Hughes testily wanted to know where his boat was. "They are bringing one out from town on a trailer," Rolvaag said. "Be here in a few minutes."

"If my boat isn't ready right now, I am going back to Iowa," Hughes fumed.

"Have a nice trip back home," Rolvaag said; then he started up his motor and left Hughes standing there.

Rolvaag was the kind of guy you had to vote for.

Going Bugs

For weeks there have been reports of robins, eagles, loons, hawks, all manner of flying critters, harbingers of summer, but last week I saw the first real, incontestable sign. I saw my first blackfly.

If there is anything that signals the coming of summer, it is that pesky little creature that goes by the alias of "sand fly" or "gnat," among printable appellations. They are on par, in the value scale, with ticks, both somewhere below the zero mark and certainly no credit to God's handiwork. On the contrary, there is good reason to believe blackflies and ticks were created in the nether world by the Forces of Darkness.

Blackflies are universally hated in the northland, not only in this area, but also across northern Wisconsin and Michigan. Once upon a time, a company in Michigan made a lotion called BF 100, which was about the only effective repellant to discourage these tiny biters from dining on one's epidermis. Only the EPA pulled BF 100 off the market because, they said, it contained some chemicals harmful to people.

No one apparently determined if blackflies were worse than the chemicals, but now BF 100 lies among the discards. You can't buy it any more. And the stuff sold in various bottles as "insect repellant" has no effect on blackflies. Indeed, as my friend Vic says, "Blackflies lap that stuff up like martinis."

Mosquitoes can be repelled, yes. There are a number of effective bottled repellants, mostly built around formulas containing a chemical called "deet." How much deet determines how well the mosquitoes stay off . . . and for how long. It works. But it does not work on blackflies. Deet martinis are preferred by blackflies. However, all is not lost. We can still swat. A good, lethal swat is not only effective but self-satisfying, particularly if the smashed insect is discovered under the swat.

And then there are the deer ticks. Hoo boy, watch out for these miniature copies of the bigger wood tick. Wood ticks bite, bury their heads under your hide, and leave a welt that itches. They can be pulled off most effectively with tweezers, gripping them as close to the skin as possible to try and get the head and all.

Deer ticks, however, carry Lyme disease, named for Lyme, Massachusetts, where they were first discovered and where we all emphatically wish they had stayed. We now have them here. Not as plentiful as the wood tick, but still enough.

Lyme disease is very debilitating. Its effects are like a combination of arthritis, flu, and a few other afflictions, all thrown together. If caught early, it can be cured with antibiotics. It must be caught early, however. The deer tick is a very tiny, somewhat reddish tick. The bite is unique in that it leaves a red ring around the puncture. Looks something like a touch of ringworm.

Anyone who spends much time outdoors should be aware of these miserable woods dwellers. Any bite that appears in the center of a red ring is suspect and should be shown to a doctor immediately.

Ticks can often be discouraged by the way clothing is worn. Long socks, boots, and pants cuffs "pegged" into the socks are effective. Shirts with long sleeves help. Some people wear rubber bands on the shirt cuffs. And watch. Look yourself over now and

then for ticks. Better yet, have a friend do it. Pull off any tick spotted. If it is a tiny one, put it in bottle and take it to the clinic for identification. But most of all, watch for that red ring.

Outside of all that, have a very pleasant and fun-filled summer. Sheesh!

Canceling Out

Seems these four guys and their sons scheduled a week's canoe trip, and at dawn, off they went with a tow to Basswood Lake. But something went wrong. They were back at the outfitters the same night. Trip over.

What happened was not easy to discover, but apparently at least one of the dads thought they were going to live in a cabin somewhere in the Boundary Waters and go fishing every day in the canoe. Of course, there are no cabins in the Boundary Waters, at least none you can rent and live in. Stay in a tent? For some folks this is simply not a viable activity.

It just happened that I was at the outfitter's having a cup of coffee when the four dads and four kids returned. Kind of a sad thing. At least for the kids. One dad said he was coming back up with his boy for another go at it. He had the idea, anyway.

Most people who book canoe trips into the BWCAW enjoy themselves. Something like 93 percent or more, according to studies made. A few don't. Usually it is the weather or bugs or both that wreck a trip. But, occasionally, something else does. Like wildlife.

Once, back in the early 1970s, when I was outfitting trips, we had two brothers from Chicago come up for a week's canoe ad-

venture. They had never been in the woods before, and we were careful to map out an easy trip, make sure all the equipment was in tip-top shape. Right after breakfast, off they went. Took the towboat to Ensign portage and went in from there. So far, so good.

At 6 A.M., the following morning, I was out in the canoe yard, getting equipment lined up for the day, and, uh oh, here were the two brothers packing clothes and fishing tackle into the trunk of their car.

Wondering what had cut the week trip down to one night and hoping my crew hadn't left out something like the tent or a sleeping bag, I wandered over. The young men did not seem particularly communicative. However, they didn't start yelling about any problems with the equipment or the food. They just kept stuffing their personal items into the car trunk.

"Cut the trip a little short?" I inquired, tentatively.

"Yeah." The older brother grunted but didn't look up.

The weather had been excellent, so I knew it couldn't be that. "Lot of bugs out there?"

"Nah," the older brother said.

"We couldn't sleep," the younger brother volunteered.

"Oh?" I was curious. "What kept you awake?"

"Animals," the older one said.

"Animals?" Right way I thought of a bear. "What kind of animals?"

"Animals that yell all night."

Now, there are not many animals that yell all night in the Boundary Waters. Wolves may howl, but that's it. This was certainly curious. "What kind of animals?" I asked.

"We don't know," the older brother said, "but it was some kind of big animals that yelled all night . . . went loo . . . loo . . . loo-oo-oo."

"Did you notice some big black and white birds on the water before you went to bed?" I asked.

"Yeah. What the heck were they?"

"They were loons. That's what was making the noise at night."

"You mean birds were doing that?"

"Yeah, loons."

They looked at me in disbelief, finished loading up the car, got in, and headed for Chicago.

As far as I know, that was the only time loons chased somebody off Ensign Lake.

Duck Stuff

When it rains, it pours, or something to that effect. Or whatever can go wrong, will, according to Murphy's Law. Two weeks ago, driving back from Babbitt at night, Andy Hill ran into a bull moose that demolished the car he was driving. Totaled it. Bad luck. Putting that behind him, what with the duck season about to open, Hill went out to his favorite slough to build a duck blind. Because of low water, he couldn't get the boat back into the area where he usually hunts, so he decided to build a blind out of poles in more open water, one that he could run the boat up into.

He cut some popple poles on his property up by Hidden Valley and hauled them out in his truck. Took them up the lake in the boat, jammed them into the mud, and wove a latticework of grass and branches into the frame. Everything was set for opening day. Saturday, just before the noon opening time, Andy, Terry Myers from Silver Rapids Lodge, and Andy's dog "Toller" motored up to the blind. Or where the blind had been. A family of beavers had dismantled most of the popple poles and hauled them off to their lodge for a winter food supply.

As far as we know, this is the first time we ever heard of a duck blind being eaten by beavers. No, they didn't get any ducks.

Ely Echoes

Butch Diesslin not only is one of the area's most avid duck hunters and a longtime sparkplug for Ducks Unlimited, but is a gourmet wild-duck cook. There are some people who shoot ducks and don't really know what to do with them after they've gotten them plucked and drawn. Some people look in a cookbook, but these are seldom satisfactory. Butch has his own style.

Thus, when an invitation arrived for a mallard duck dinner at Butch and Lucy's house, there was no hesitation in accepting. Didn't even have to look at the calender. If there was a conflict, whatever else was on the calender would have to take a back seat.

The mallards were excellent. Near as I can remember, here is how Butch fixed 'em. First, he makes sure the ducks are completely cleaned right after he kills 'em. To scrub every last bit of blood out of the body cavity, he uses an old toothbrush. At least, I assumed it was an old toothbrush. You never know about duck hunters.

For cooking, the body cavity is salted and peppered, given a dash of garlic salt, stuffed with an onion or an apple, and placed in the oven to bake for a couple of hours at 275 degrees. Now, this is critical, Butch points out. Wild ducks take a long time to cook. They should be cooked so the meat can be pulled off the bones with a fork. Most game recipes don't insist on this, but it is a key item. Wild rice was a side dish. We demolished it all.

My wife, Lil, used to use a similar system, except she placed a peeled orange in each body cavity and basted the birds with orange juice. Then she took the juice from the bottom of the roaster and made orange gravy, which went over the wild rice and the sliced duck.

The only way wild duck can be cooked wrong is not cooked enough.

Opening Day

Cousin Willie and I went out on the walleye opener. Willie is an Ely summer-home owner from Aurora, Illinois. He isn't much for ice-fishing, so the spring opener is a pretty heavy deal with him. Willie figures ice fishermen are all mentally challenged. Learning impaired, maybe. They don't start out that way, but they get their brains frostbit. Willie prefers fishing in open water. It was open on opening day, Saturday. The solunar tables said peak fishing was 10:10 A.M. We were on the water at 7 A.M.

Willie: What're we riggin' with?

Me: Minnows.

Willie: Just minnows?

Me: Jigs and minnows, for Pete's sake.

Willie: I got some jigs here in the tackle box.

Me: Good. Tie on one.

Willie: Toss me a minnow.

Me: Here. Catch.

Willie: I think I got a bite.

Me: You probably got the bottom.

Willie: The bottom is swimming away with my minnow.

Me: Set the hook.

Willie: It's a pretty good one.

Me : Ain't no walleye.

Willie: Whatta ya mean?

Me: It's a big-toothed, green, weed shark.

Willie: Are we keepin' northern pike?

Me: Nuh.

Willie: Gimmie 'nother minnow.

Me: We shoulda brought a thermos of coffee.

Willie: I got 'nother bite.

Me: Probably got the bottom.

Willie: This is a bigger bottom than the last bottom.

Me: Looks like 'nother pike.

Willie: Nope, it's a walleye.

Me: Geez, lemme net it.

Willie: Toss me 'nother minnow.

Me: Coming up.

Willie: I got 'nother bite.

Me: What kinda jig are you using?

Willie: I dunno. Kinda green.

Me: I think I got a green one in my tackle box.

Willie: I got another walleye.

Me: Land it yourself.

Willie: Throw me another minnow.

Me: Not until I catch a walleye.

Willie: That's lousy.

Me: Who said fishing is fair?

(Two hours later the score stood: Willie 4, me 2.)

Willie: It's starting to cloud up.

Me: We got enough. We're outta here.

Willie: You said you were big on catch and release.

Me: Right.

Willie: How come we got six walleyes on the stringer?

Me: Right. Catch and release. We are gonna release these fish into the frying pan.

(For the record: We didn't get a lot, but the walleyes we caught were in shallow water, from three to six feet down. They hit lightly and we missed some strikes by setting the hook too quick. Yeah, we do practice catch and release. But when the season first opens, we just gotta have some fish to eat if we can catch 'em.)

P.S: We ate 'em.

Some Thoughts on Fishing

Nothing beats fishing with kids. There is something about seeing kids catch fish that sort of makes us relive our own early fishing days.

Within the past couple of weeks I was lucky enough to go fishing with two sets of kids. The first were Matt and Josh Dayton, sons of Gene Dayton, whose family has a summer place on Jasper Lake. Matt, age fifteen, a junior Olympic ski champion and well on his way to becoming a U.S. ski team member, was in my canoe. His brother Josh, age five, was in a canoe with his dad.

We got lucky on Basswood and started to nail some fish. In the middle of this ruckus, Josh tied into a pretty good-sized pike. His dad was giving him instructions: "Keep the rod tip up, keep the line tight." You know the routine.

Well, little Josh was fighting that pike with all his might, and he had the rod tip up. Only the line got wrapped around the tip or something. The pike make a great rush, bent the rod over, and broke rod and line at the same time, leaving Josh holding the rod handle with just the reel. But we had a great day and caught a good fish fry for the folks back at the cabin.

The second trip was with my cousin Bill Paull, from Illinois, and his grandson Frankie, who is ten. Frankie is a dedicated angler, reading everything he can get his hands on about fishing, watching all the outdoor TV shows, and fishing whenever the chance appears. High point of his summer is coming up to Ely for the annual fishing trip. Again, we were on Basswood, and once again the fish were cooperating.

We were on the edge of a rocky reef where a herd of bass were trying to commit hari kari. Cousin Bill was in the bow, Frankie in the center seat, and me in the stern. Frankie had just busted a big bass, and I had laid down my rod to land his fish. When I picked the rod up again, the hook was stuck on the rocky reef about fifty feet away.

"S'matter?" Frankie asked.

"Got snagged," I said, laying the rod across the canoe gunwale and reaching for the anchor rope. I gave a good heave on the rope to pull the anchor free from the bottom, but instead of the anchor moving, it stayed stuck in the rocks and the canoe jerked backward. With that, the line went tight and my rod jumped over the side and into the lake.

Frankie watched the rod sink and gave me a worried look. "Whatcha gonna do?"

"Gonna get it back," I said. "Gimme your rod and I'll snag my line."

Frankie looked very doubtful, but I knew where the rod was and the line that stretched from the sunken rod to the rock pile. It took about five minutes of dragging Frankie's hook along the bottom, but eventually I hooked my line and pulled up the rod and reel.

"That's pretty cool," Frankie said.

"When you have fished as long as I have, Frank," I told him,"
you have done about everything wrong you possibly can, so you
learn how to correct your mistakes."

Fortunately, the fish kept right on biting. After we had enough
bass and walleyes for supper, we went on and caught about a dozen
or so nice walleyes and released them. That is, Frankie and I did.
Cousin Bill was having some difficulty, a situation Frankie noted
quickly.

"Grandpa, you got to get your bait right down to the bottom,"
Frankie said.

"Grandpa, maybe you ought to try a leech instead of a worm."

"Grandpa. Maybe you should be using an orange jig like I
am."

Cousin Bill liked to split laughing. "You are now an expert,"
he said.

"When are you going to write your book on fishing?" I asked.

"Well, maybe one of these days," Frankie said, seriously.

"What are you going to call the book?" I asked.

"Cool Fishing," Frank said.

Can't beat that.

It was former President Herb Hoover who noted that "all men are
equal before the fish." Herb was a lot better fisherman than he
was a politician. You've got to be pretty old to remember when
Herb Hoover was President. Nineteen-twenty-eight. He had a
lousy time because that was when the thing called the Great Depression broke out. All across the world. But Herb got blamed for
it in this country.

However, he did like to fish, and he was smart enough to understand that fish don't really care who you are or what your sta-
tus in life may be. They bite when they want, and they don't care

how much your tackle or your boat or boots cost. And they may not bite at all. Which is where the thread of this story begins.

Earlier this year, about the time when the ice went out, the Rev. Mike DeArruda, one Sunday, commented from the pulpit that although he had lived in Ely for a couple of years and had been fishing several times, he had never caught any of our local fish. Being impulsive and also somewhat defensive when it comes to Ely angling, I invited him to go fishing on Opening Day with the promise: "You'll get some walleyes . . . I'll guarantee it."

Any fisherman in his right mind knows you never guarantee anything, but not many of us are in our right minds or we probably wouldn't be fishermen in the first place. Perhaps, subconsciously, I was looking for a little insurance. You know, if a man of the cloth goes along, maybe the Almighty would exert some influence on how the fish bite. That, in itself, is a poor assumption and certainly theologically unsound.

Anyway, the walleyes WERE biting on Opening Day; but it so happened that Mike had to attend some church meeting out east and missed. So when he got back, we set up another trip. It was during a recent hot spell, but it didn't seem like that should bother the fish much. In any event, we got to my favorite lake, put in the canoe, and started out. First shot out of the box, I nailed a walleye. Small, but an eater. I smiled. Hoo, boy. It looked like it was going to be one of those great days. But that walleye was it. End of story. We didn't get anything else worth putting on the stringer. By noon, we couldn't even get a perch to bite. Zip. I do not know if Mike offered any prayers for divine assistance or not. At least, he didn't say any out loud.

Anyway, it's like Herb Hoover pointed out. The fish don't care who you are.

The Best Kind of Work

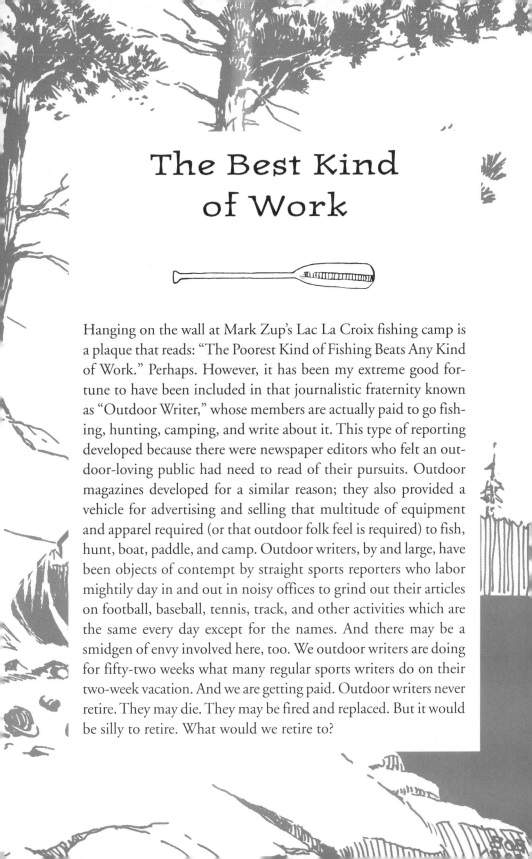

Hanging on the wall at Mark Zup's Lac La Croix fishing camp is a plaque that reads: "The Poorest Kind of Fishing Beats Any Kind of Work." Perhaps. However, it has been my extreme good fortune to have been included in that journalistic fraternity known as "Outdoor Writer," whose members are actually paid to go fishing, hunting, camping, and write about it. This type of reporting developed because there were newspaper editors who felt an outdoor-loving public had need to read of their pursuits. Outdoor magazines developed for a similar reason; they also provided a vehicle for advertising and selling that multitude of equipment and apparel required (or that outdoor folk feel is required) to fish, hunt, boat, paddle, and camp. Outdoor writers, by and large, have been objects of contempt by straight sports reporters who labor mightily day in and out in noisy offices to grind out their articles on football, baseball, tennis, track, and other activities which are the same every day except for the names. And there may be a smidgen of envy involved here, too. We outdoor writers are doing for fifty-two weeks what many regular sports writers do on their two-week vacation. And we are getting paid. Outdoor writers never retire. They may die. They may be fired and replaced. But it would be silly to retire. What would we retire to?

My Friend the Duck Hunter

My Friend the Duck Hunter from up the lake always blamed me for his divorce because I was the guy who introduced him to duck hunting. This was in days of yore, when the hunting endeavor became his chief obsession, resulting in long absences from home, etc., a situation that is not conducive to matrimonial harmony. However, I have never entirely accepted the theory that duck hunting was the problem. It may have been a contributing cause, but this and other matters led to other rifts and disputes that eventually resulted in a parting of ways.

This matter has always been somewhat of a burden on my soul since both of the parties involved are nice people. Duck hunters say that duck hunting does strange things to those who pursue the sport with single-minded fervor. Well, that is only partially correct, because duck hunting is not a sport, either. It is an addiction, nearly incurable at that.

Anyway, My Friend the Duck Hunter has labored through these several years with this addiction, a broken marriage and what all. (Fortunately, the former wife found an upstanding new spouse and is embarked on a new life.)

Sometime back, I wrote that the Duck Hunter met an attractive new friend of the female gender who was visiting here in Ely and he asked her for a date. What he proposed was a day-long trip into the Boundary Waters. Only he didn't really explain that what he wanted to do was build a new duck blind and he needed an extra set of hands to cut swamp grass, weave in brush, and so on.

So off they went, up the lake, to the swamp and the duck blind site. This type of venture is not normally conducive to a long-lasting romantic relationship. However, the young lady took it all in stride and even indicated some measure of interest in just what the heck they were doing out on the soggy margin of a swamp, putting up a framework of tree limbs, adding brush and weeds.

One might agree that this is a rather forceful way of determining if someone has any type of interest in the outdoors, and duck hunting in particular. It is certainly not recommended as an overall romantic pursuit. However, the friendship endured, even thrived, over many months, and eventually culminated in marriage a week ago in the Caribbean.

Admittedly, the Caribbean is a far cry from a duck blind in the northland, but what was going on was this: See, My Friend the Duck Hunter has a waterfowl-hunting acquaintance who owns a small resort operation on an island in the Caribbean. That is, he did until the last hurricane screeched through and blew it into the salt water. Being of kind nature and particularly congenial toward others with a waterfowl addiction, My Friend the D. H. and his bride-to-be flew down there and proceeded to help rebuild the resort over a period of weeks.

Possibly inspired by the colorful setting in that tropical paradise, the two visitors from the north determined to tie the knot, then and there. Wedding vows were said in an island church, and the reception was held on one of the few watercraft still afloat after the hurricane—a one-hundred-foot cement barge. Apparently everything went well, and the festivities were enjoyed by all. The Duck Hunter and his new bride are heading home imbued with connubial bliss.

Does the new bride intend to take up the sport of duck hunting next fall? This is currently an unknown. However, I do know that it is a sign of a solid marriage when a man is brave enough to go into the wilds accompanied by a woman carrying a loaded shotgun, particularly if the woman is his wife.

Remembering Charles

Last Tuesday, they laid Charles Kuralt away at Chapel Hill in his home state of North Carolina. Hard to find anyone in the U.S. who didn't know Charles Kuralt from CBS television. He had another career as an author and a third one as owner of the Ely radio station WELY. It was my stroke of good fortune to have met with Mr. Kuralt a couple of times, talking "shop" as one newsman to another. He related how he started out as a writer for the Charlotte, North Carolina, newspaper and then got picked up by CBS, which was expanding its news department back then with people like Edward R. Murrow and Walter Cronkite.

One of Kuralt's first assignments was to cover the Vietnam war. "I made it through one tour of duty there," Kuralt said. "And when I got back to New York, I told CBS that I was not going to take any more such assignments. I would quit first. They asked what the problem was, and I told them that a battlefield is no place for a short, fat guy who can't run."

More than anything, the nation—and Ely—will miss his quiet good humor. Fortunately, on tape, we can still hear that marvelous voice inviting people to Ely "at the end of the road."

From Birdshot

A reporter for the *St. Paul Pioneer Press* was in the Chamber of Commerce office last week. Came up to do an article on how awful everybody in Ely must feel about the long winter and all that stuff. She got an awful shock. "Hey, you are in winter country, now," Linda Fryer told her. "We had the greatest winter for recreation ever."

"But how about this late ice-out. How does this affect everybody?" the reporter asked.

Barb DeToffol had just walked in the office. "If you think people have long faces up here, you're wrong," she said. "What we are doing out on Shagawa Lake is this: We have all the resort people building big bonfires, and we are going to melt the ice off before the walleye opener."

The *Pioneer Press* reporter was busy writing like the dickens. Then she stopped and looked up. "Are you kidding me?"

The *Echo* writer had just walked in. "No, we never kid anybody," he said. "Outside of Shagawa with the bonfires, we are looking forward to a lot of the frozen lakes with anticipation. We get to use two poles on the walleye opener, fishing through the ice."

"Is that legal?" the reporter asked.

"Through the ice, yes. In open water you can use only one pole," Linda said.

"Well, when do you expect the ice to go off?"

"We check with Fernberg Freddie, our pet groundhog," the *Echo* writer said, "to find out how deep the frost is. You have heard of Puxatawney Phil out in Ohio, the groundhog who comes up to see his shadow?"

The *Pioneer Press* lady allowed she had.

"Well, up here," the *Echo* writer continued, "we usually have three or four feet of snow cover on Groundhog Day. What we do, as soon as the snow goes, is have one of the doctors from the clinic go out and check on Freddie down in his den."

"How does he do that?" the *Pioneer Press* reporter asked.

"He takes along a proctoscope and pushes it down the hole until he locates the groundhog. Then he checks to see how far down in the ground he is. Last week, he had moved another foot deeper."

It will be interesting to see what appears in the *Pioneer Press*.

Pond Singers

They come out about as soon as the ice is off for good, the days are warm, and the grass starts to green up . . . the Hyla crucifers. Little Hyla crucifers. There are lots of Hylas, but the ones we have around here are teeny weenies, although they make a lot of noise for their size.

Spring peepers. The little brownish-gray frogs that appear as if by magic in every roadside ditch, beaver pond, flooded woodland low spot, marsh, creek bottom . . . wherever it is wet in the spring. Up here, peepers are the earliest frogs to appear, and their songs rattle through the woodlands in a merry chorus unlike any other. These fascinating little critters are difficult to see until they sing, when the vocal sac swells out like bubble gum. If you walk toward the sound, they will shut up. But if you sit down alongside the water and remain still for awhile, one, then two, then the rest will begin their staccato calling. Remaining still, you may look closely for the white vocal sac, and if the water is still, tiny ripples emanating from the frog will pinpoint its location as it calls at the top of it lungs.

The second part of the name, "crucifer," applies to a tiny, irregular cross on its back. After the eggs are laid and fertilized, the

teensy tadpoles hatch out and scramble around to eat all manner of minute life. By the end of summer the baby frogs, about the size of a housefly, can be found in the muddy shallows. They feed on insects such as mosquitos, and scientists say they can jump seventeen times their own length to grab a meal.

But one does not have to be a scientist to simply sit and enjoy the chorus of spring peepers. Lots of other things inhabit the same muddy shorelines: shorebirds, dragonflies, turtles, snakes, all manner of fascinating dwellers. Overhead, mallards circle, quacking at each other, and woodpeckers yammer on nearby dead trees. White-throated sparrows call from the forest understory. What a time to look and listen!

Late Autumn Symphony

Hill: Hey, the crappies are hitting up on Basswood. You wanna go?

Me: I got a lot of stuff to do. You're sure they are biting?

Hill: Man, they are killing 'em. I was up with Steve Piragis last week. Got some slabs. Like pie plates.

(So it was that on Sunday morning, Andy Hill, Jeff Nosbisch, and I set out for Basswood Lake. The wind was blowing—maybe howling is a better word. We pulled the boat across at Prairie Portage, using a slick set of wheels Hill had invented, then banged and boomed through the waves past Bailey Bay, Merriam Bay, and Frog Bay, our vertebrae getting jammed on the boat seats. Eventually, we got to what Hill identified as the crappie hole. The wind was now screeching, and we couldn't hold the boat.)

Hill: We gotta find a big rock for an anchor.

Jeff: Right. Get over to the shore and I'll get us a rock.

Me: A big one.

(Jeff found a boulder that he wrestled to the bow of the boat and lashed onto a section of rope. We went out into the waves.)

Hill: Help yourself to the minnows.

Me: My fingers are freezing. I can't hold onto them.

Jeff: How far down you fishing?

Hill: Let the line down to the bottom and raise it up a little.

Me: Anybody bring a fish locator so we can tell where the crappies are hanging out?

Hill: Mine's busted.

Jeff: I don't own one.

(Two hours went by without a bite.)

Jeff: I don't think they're biting.

Hill: Maybe we should try another spot.

Me: Yeah...like in front of the TV watching the football game.

Hill: See if you can get the anchor up.

Jeff: I think it sunk into the mud.

Hill: We can't go until we get the rock off the bottom.

(Jeff heaved and hauled, and finally the anchor came off the bottom. He pulled it up and untied it, and we were on our way. The wind had gotten windier, if that was possible. The boat slammed and smashed its way to Prairie Portage. We slid on the portage wheels and pulled it up the hill to Sucker Lake.)

Hill: Maybe we could get a couple of walleyes on the way back.

Jeff: Do we have to?

Me: What's to lose? We're already up here.

Jeff: And frozen.

(We anchored over a hole out of the wind, behind an island on Sucker Lake, and with shaking fingers, baited up. Believe it or not, we managed to scrounge up seven walleyes. Enough so we each had supper.)

Hill: Enough's enough. We're outta here.

Jeff: I didn't think you'd ever say it.

(I couldn't say anything. I was afraid to open my mouth. My teeth were rattling so bad they might get the enamel chipped. When we finally got home, stiff and wet, the football games were on. Denver was playing San Francisco. Inside the cabin it was warm. I fell asleep on the couch. The telephone ringing woke me up.)

Hill: Hey, how you doing?

Me: I don't want to go crappie fishing.

Hill: No, I wondered what you were going to do during deer season . . . maybe we oughta get out and scout the woods.

Me: For the love of Pete, Andy, deer season is two weeks away.

Hill: Yeah, but we oughta go scout out the woods.

Me: Yeah-h-h. Tell you what. Don't call me, I'll call you.

(I went back to sleep on the couch. I don't have any idea who won the football game, but I wondered if there is some way I could haul the couch to the deer stand on opening day and stretch out there in a warm sleeping bag. Deer hunting is a cold, sometimes dreary pursuit, but at least you don't have to stick your hands in ice water looking for minnows.)

The Ahlgrens

Along the roadways, purple and pale blue asters were arrayed in clumps, interspersed with yellow ragweed and the whitish heads of pearly everlasting. It was while absorbed in these fall flowers that I chanced upon Cliff and Isabel Ahlgren, taking one of their daily walks. As a neophyte flower student, I remarked upon the two types of asters I had observed, a statement that elicited a hearty laugh. Not two, they informed me, but fifteen types of asters dwell in the Boundary Waters area. (They still look like two to me).

The Ahlgrens, lest time dims the memory, were the two accomplished scientists who managed the Wilderness Research Center established by Frank Hubachek on Basswood Lake nearly a half century ago. Over time, the Ahlgrens and their students helped gather and catalogue over 500 species of plants. Currently, Cliff and Isabel are videotaping the area's wildflowers and have some 250 on film. Cliff does the photography, Isabel is handling the narration. Once the film is edited, it will be put on a CD and become available for anyone interested in north country wildflowers.

A few years back, Cliff and Isabel published a remarkable book called *Lob Trees of the Wilderness*. It relates information they found while overseeing a huge staff of researchers for forty-five years.

Included in their work, and perhaps most important, are studies of white pine. At the urging of other scientists, they embarked on a program of gathering seeds from white pines resistent to the deadly blister rust, planting them, and monitoring the results. From these plantings, more seeds were recovered and planted. Also, grafts were made from pines that appeared rust-resistant. The goal was to use Boundary Waters stock to develop white pines that would not be killed by the disease.

Of course, the Research Center has been long gone from Basswood Lake, but the thousands of trees the staff planted are still growing. "We went up there this summer," Isabel noted, "and looked at some of those early plantings. The pines are now eighteen feet tall and underneath are growing more pines springing up from seed."

"I almost cried when I saw them," she added. "They are like my grandchildren."

In years to come, probably few people will know that those impressive stands of white and Norway pines were planted on old resort sites by people. Future wilderness travelers will no doubt remark on the ingenuity of Mother Nature, creating those impressive stands of tall trees.

Cliff laughed when recalling that when Jack Ford, the President's son, visited the Center with a reporter in 1978, they hiked to the top of a ridge, where they could view the forest spreading out below. The reporter pointed out several stands of large pines, indicating to Jack Ford that it was such natural stands of native trees that the 1978 legislation was aimed at preserving. When Cliff pointed out that he had personally planted those pines many years before, the writer fell into embarrassed silence.

Anyone who has a real interest in a scientific study of Boundary Waters flora can gain considerable insight from *Lob Trees in the Wilderness*. Local stores usually carry the book, but if one can-

not be located, the Ahlgrens have a supply themselves. They are spending the summer on Moose Lake, but will be heading south with the ducks and geese when fall arrives. And they have promised to let us know when they have the wildflower CD completed and available.

A Man Named Stanley Owl

Stanley said he was a Huron, from up in the Nipigon River country of Ontario, but he spent most of his adult life guiding anglers in the border waters of northern Minnesota and Ontario, in the land of the Ojibwe. Stan said he had a lot of Ojibwe relatives and when he wasn't guiding, he could be found on one reservation or another, hanging out. We first met Stan back in the early 1950s, up in the Crooked Lake country, an area that he came to know quite intimately and where his guiding skills became legendary.

It was the spring of 1959. We were at Billy Zup's Curtain Falls Camp, which in those days was located at the outlet of Crooked Lake, where the waters churn in a thundering, frothy cascade into Iron Lake. That evening Stanley had returned from successfully guiding two anglers to the clear, trout-filled waters of Brent Lake, farther north. Supper was over, and the two anglers were leaning on the polished wood bar, reminiscing over their adventure.

"You know Stanley Owl?" the tall one asked me.

"Sure. Known Stanley for some time. Why?"

"We just got back from an overnight trip with Stanley up to Brent," the short one put in. "He said something kinda funny."

"How's that?" I asked.

"We got a late start the first day," the tall one noted. "And with five portages we didn't get up to Brent Lake until almost dark. Anyhow, Stanley got the tent up, the air mattresses blown up, and the sleeping bags laid out. We hustled up a stack of firewood, then cooked supper. It was a pretty nice meal for being 'way up there, with T-bones broiled over the open fire, potatoes baked in foil, and sweet corn. Anyhow, when we got supper over it was dark and time to turn in."

"We not only had air mattresses under our sleeping bags," the short guy added, "but we had some kind of inflatable air pillows, which Stanley blew up. He had a candle in the tent and in the candlelight we climbed into our sleeping bags for the night. I don't know why—maybe out of habit or something—but as I slid into my sleeping bag, I reached into my pants pocket, pulled out my billfold, and tucked it under my pillow.

"About this time, Stanley raised up on his elbows and looked at me for moment. Then just before he blew out the candle he said: 'You don't have to hide your billfold . . . there's not another white man within forty miles of here.' "

I recall seeing Stanley up at Billy's camp, one October, a time when the aspen were turning to gold, the maples were like spots of flame against the blue-green spruce and fir, ducks were flying, and fall fishing was at a fever pitch. We had come in on horseback, up the old Lac La Croix Trail, horse wrangler Wayne Berry, Ralph Smith, and myself. We had spent a memorable day on the water, socking into dozens of trophy-sized walleyes and then finishing up in the Big Current at the head of Crooked Lake, with two dozen catch-and-release smallmouth bass from three to six pounds.

We attempted to hit Billy Zup at suppertime with a barrage of stories concerning our angling adventure, but he appeared considerably preoccupied. Then as darkness settled down, his brow furrowed with worry.

"Wished those kids were back," he groaned.

"What kids . . . back from where," we asked.

"My two boys, Patty and Billy Jr., went duck hunting by themselves up on the Beartrap River today . . . should have been back before supper . . . now it's pitch dark and they must have gotten lost."

Although just teenagers, young Pat and Billy were good in the woods, good enough to stop and build a fire if they lost the trail. Still, the Beartrap River lay in a vast, seldom-visited piece of wilderness, and the father's concern was understandable.

Stanley had just come in from supper in the cook shack, sized up the situation, and offered to go get the two boys.

"How are you going to find them?" Wayne asked.

"I know where they went," Stan said, slipping on his jacket.

"You want a lantern?" Bill asked.

"Nope." Stan zipped up the jacket and vanished into the night.

There wasn't much talk in the lodge as the hours went by and old Bill paced up and down with worry. Wayne, Ralph, and I read magazines, talked softy about the next day's fishing, and glanced at our watches from time to time. About a half hour before midnight, the outside door creaked and Stanley strode in, followed by two tired and disheveled young duck hunters. As the relieved father hustled the kids off to the kitchen for some supper, Stanley flipped off his jacket and cradled a hot mug of coffee.

"Where'd you find 'em, Stan?" Wayne asked.

"Over along the river . . . they went the wrong way where the trail forked, but they had enough sense to stop and build a fire."

"That was a pretty good trick, Stan," I said.

"How's that?"

"Well . . . going all that way in the pitch dark and locating those two kids. How'd you know where to look?"

Stanley took a long sip of coffee." Well . . . you just know."

"I've never seen you use a compass or a map," I persisted.

"No. Stanley doesn't need a compass or a map."

"You ever been lost?"

Stan looked at me and laughed. "Nope."

"Never?"

"Never." He finished off the coffee and grinned broadly. "Couple of times my canoe got lost. Couple of times my camp got lost; but Stanley never got lost." He aimed a brown finger at his boots. "Stanley is always standing right here."

Some Travel
by Dogsled

Hike! Hike!

The sound of mushers urging their dog teams to hit the trail, the barking and baying of huskies, Indian dogs, and all varieties in-between, signals the start of the winter trout season on the border lakes. Saturday, January 3, was the official opener on trout lakes wholly within the Boundary Waters, and while snow in the woods was not as heavy as one might wish, the lakes were frozen and snow-packed and the surfaces fast.

It isn't the fish. If it was just the fish, nobody would be out with sled dogs or on skis. We would simply shop at IGA or Zup's and buy our fish. It is the aura, the excitement of participating in a winter wilderness trip under some of nature's most trying circumstances that draws us.

Winter fishing is, in many respects, a test of one's manhood or womanhood. There is an old saying about the wilderness: "If you make a mistake in the summer and dump your canoe, you may get wet and bug-bitten, but if you make a mistake in the winter, you may become a headline."

And there is another saying: "In the winter, there are no B-pluses, only straight A's." Both sayings are true.

Part of the challenge of winter activities is testing oneself against the elements. There is always an underlying, small sense of danger, that possibility of an unheralded blizzard that could blot out the world or an overnight temperature drop to a searing 40 or 50 below. But with proper clothing and equipment and a measure of know-how, the element of risk takes a far back seat to the exhilaration, the sheer beauty of it all.

There is an acute sense of excitement that infects any group starting out at daybreak on the glistening, snow-packed surface of an icebound lake. On very cold days, a purplish-white mist hovers over the low spots, adding a coat of frost to the aspen and birch trees jutting up over the dark green spruce and fir. The sun does not come up with a white flash of brilliance, as in summer. Instead, it slides up sort of sideways, through the tree screen to the east, an red-orange blob that is accompanied by the thumping and groaning of lake ice expanding and shifting. Puffs of vapor appear around everyone's parka hood and around the muzzles of the harnessed dogs, eager to get going. Overhead a few ravens wing their way on a never-ending search for food, their guttural croaks sharp and clear in the still air. A Canada jay drifts down softly, beady black eyes scouring the scene for perhaps a crust of bread, a bit of cracker.

"Hike! Hike!' With the hook up, the musher pushes off, the dogs straining at the harness, sled runners creaking on the cold snow. All of the gear (and sometimes a passenger) are securely folded within the basket of the sled. The trail down the lake is starkly interspersed with bright ribbons of sunlight and long fingers of blue shadow cast by the shoreline trees.

Within the woods, showers of tiny frost crystals, loosened from the tree branches, cascade like streamers of diamond dust to the blanketed forest floor. Sometimes those of us skiing behind the dog teams simply stop in awe and try to take in the immensity of the scene. To the north, east, south, and west, snow stretches unbroken to the blue-green, forested hills. Beyond the hills lie more snow-capped lakes and more wooded ridges unmarred by highways, shopping centers, townhouse developments, or other accoutrements of civilization.

If we happen to luck out and catch some trout, that's a notable plus. But it isn't a tight requirement. Just being out there is enough. Hike! Hike!

First Come,
First Served

The thump of furtive footsteps on the front deck was followed by a crash. Thoroughly awakened, I flipped on the bed lamp. One A.M., barefoot and pajama-clad, I dashed to the living room and turned on the porch light. Two bears of about 250 pounds each, one black, one brown, were in the process of dismantling the large bird feeder that formerly hung from the eaves.

"Scat! Git!" was all it took to get the bears in motion. They shuffled off into the dark. I retrieved my battered feeder. Another episode in a thirty-year saga of living with bears.

Every fall we northern Minnesotans have bears in the news; but in a year like this one, with a failed blueberry crop and a lack of hazelnuts, hungry bears become much more apparent. Bears invade the city outskirts, raiding garbage cans. Where I live, on the upper rim of the Superior National Forest, I have more bear neighbors than human. My home is in the middle of what some folks might call a "bear problem area." It depends upon one's viewpoint.

Veteran conservation officer Bob Jacobsen, now retired, once told me: "People consider bears as invaders, but if you look at it from the standpoint of the bears, we are the invaders. The bears were here first."

Put in that perspective, bears assume a somewhat different identity. Their depredations are simply a matter of natural instincts. They are hungry and go where they detect food. By mid-August, they had detected food in my raspberry patch, a rather lush crop for so dry a year. Overnight not only was the patch stripped of berries, but half the stalks were beaten to the ground. Fortunately, I had already harvested several gallons of fruit and processed into enough raspberry jam for the entire year and I did not begrudge the bears a share.

Some Haralson apples are now ripening, providing a test of nerves between the bears and me. Which of us first decides that the apples are ripe enough to harvest will determine who gets them. Unfortunately, bears do not simply pluck apples from the trees. They tear down the limbs to get the fruit within reach. Three of my trees over the last five years have been totally destroyed by bears.

Ely neighbor Dr. Lynn Rogers, a noted North American bear authority, says black bears are not aggressive. They don't attack people like grizzlies may. But they are strong and can become cantankerous if attacked. The Labrador retriever of my friend Larry Rom once tangled with a bear and let out a yowl for help. Larry came charging up, saw the bear had his pet dog by the head, and unloaded a healthy kick to the bear's rear end. The bear went after Larry, knocking him down and ripping his legs, which required some skilled stitching to repair.

Black bears have the equipment to do extensive damage, although their inclination is to live and let live. And they are persistent. The two bears that took down my bird feeder were back the following night to clean up the sunflower seeds that were scat-

tered around . . . and possibly to see if I was dumb enough to put the feeder back up.

Sorry, no more free lunch. In another month and a half they will be going into hibernation, and the bird feeder can go back up. Of course, the squirrels will get into it then, but I expect that. The squirrels were here before I was, too.

Ringing in the New

Slowly they filtered into the gaily decorated dining hall of the nursing home. Some limped in with canes, some shuffled in with the aid of walkers, assisted by smiling volunteers, and the balance were wheeled in. A few laughed and chatted with each other and attendants. But most just sat silently.

It was the annual nursing home New Year's Eve party. Four of us had volunteered to provide music. Bonnie Starkman, who runs a flower and seed store, arranged her music on the piano. Former school teacher Byron Moren tuned up his string bass. Retired school staffer Ron Bronkowski fingered the valves on his trumpet. This aging writer sat on a stool behind his drums.

Byron's wife, Alice, had organized the celebration and asked us if we could play. It would be in the afternoon, she pointed out, and would not interfere with any party plans we might have for the evening. New Year's at the nursing home, Alice said, would be rung in at 3 P.M. since none of the patients were up to seeing 1997 come in at midnight. No one in the band had a problem.

About sixty nursing home patients were assembled. Some we recognized painfully as people we had known from years past. Not so long ago they had been productive members of our home

town, holding down jobs, managing businesses, active in church and community activities, busy with homes and families. Now they were largely infirm, victims of diabetes, of strokes, of aging. Many were now alone, frail, resigned, not happy over what fate had dealt them. Their eyes told it all, eyes that followed us as we arranged our music and set up to play. Some of the eyes stared at us intently. Others appeared uninterested. Some just stared into space.

Bonnie stuck a chord and we sailed into a chorus of "Embraceable You," an old standard from the 1940s. Following was an upbeat number titled "Ain't She Sweet," then "Stardust." Ron's mellow trumpet filled the room as aged fingers began tapping on tables, and here and there toes kept time on the floor. With "Tea For Two" eyes focused and began to light up. The "Beer Barrel Polka" even brought a few to their feet, and they executed some dance steps. Perhaps they held memories of dances past, of years ago when they were young and whirled around dance floors with equally young partners.

Requests came for some old songs, and we obliged. Lips moved as the words came back. Volunteers passed among the tables, handing out party hats and noisemakers along with sandwiches, coffee, and punch. At 3 P.M., Alice Moren declared that it was New Year's Eve, and we concluded with "Auld Lang Syne."

Outside, a bitter wind whipped gusts of snow across the walks and against the windows. But inside, Bonnie, Ron, Byron, and I experienced an incredible warmth. "Should auld acquaintance be forgot . . . ?"

Never.

The Ferocious
Finn Found

If there is something you need to know around Ely, simply ask the right person. If you can find him. Or her. A week or so back we ran a little piece about the "Ferocious Finn" fishing lure, a large, shiny spoon that Jim Pluth brought in. The question we asked in the *Echo* was, "Who was the Ferocious Finn?"

Who walks into the *Echo* office last week but Lyman Childers, who has a pretty good handle on what happened around Ely for the last few decades, particularly where it relates to fishing.

The Ferocious Finn, says Lyman, was a guy named Art Forselius, who ran a hardware store in Ely, about where Bobby John's is now, and also sold fishing tackle. He made those metal lures and sold them in his store. "Forselius invented the spoon that later became famous as the 'Daredevle,'" Lyman said. "Only he didn't patent it." Somebody else did and made a fortune on it.

Living in the Land of the Ojibwe

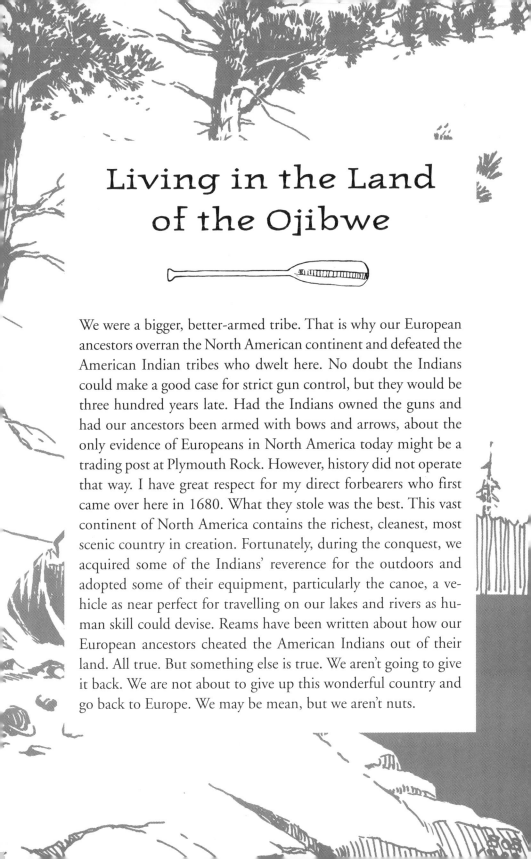

We were a bigger, better-armed tribe. That is why our European ancestors overran the North American continent and defeated the American Indian tribes who dwelt here. No doubt the Indians could make a good case for strict gun control, but they would be three hundred years late. Had the Indians owned the guns and had our ancestors been armed with bows and arrows, about the only evidence of Europeans in North America today might be a trading post at Plymouth Rock. However, history did not operate that way. I have great respect for my direct forbearers who first came over here in 1680. What they stole was the best. This vast continent of North America contains the richest, cleanest, most scenic country in creation. Fortunately, during the conquest, we acquired some of the Indians' reverence for the outdoors and adopted some of their equipment, particularly the canoe, a vehicle as near perfect for travelling on our lakes and rivers as human skill could devise. Reams have been written about how our European ancestors cheated the American Indians out of their land. All true. But something else is true. We aren't going to give it back. We are not about to give up this wonderful country and go back to Europe. We may be mean, but we aren't nuts.

G.G.

To an assortment of great-grandchildren she has always been "G.G." Great-Grandmother Cornelia. To my sister, brother-in law, wife, and me, she is Mom, but a rather unusual Mom by any measure. As this was being written, the family was preparing for her 105th birthday.

Mom was born on August 21, 1894, when Grover Cleveland was President. She lived to see the United States change from horse-drawn transportation to the family car. She took an airplane ride when the first barnstorming pilots toured the nation after World War I, marveled at television, space travel, and the incredible sight of a man walking on the moon. She lived through two world wars and several "conflicts," innumerable politicians, good and bad, and she gave birth to four children, two of whom grew to adulthood.

When she was seventy-four, my father died of emphysema and complications from a broken hip. Up to that time, she had never driven a car, Dad being firmly in charge of transportation. It was shortly after Dad broke his hip that my brother-in-law Howie, a high school coach and driver's education teacher, received a phone call at school.

"Howie," the firm, unmistakable voice on the other end announced. "I am at the Chevy dealer and have just bought a car. When school ends come out here and show me how to drive the thing."

Howie found Mom sitting impatiently in her used sedan, waiting. After a couple of training sessions in the school parking lot, she graduated to the streets, breezed through her state driving tests, and got her license on the first try. She drove until she was in her nineties, finally deciding that perhaps her reflexes were slowing up and she might become a hazard on the highways.

Up to age one hundred, she lived in her own apartment, attended church, volunteered for charitable organizations, and played tournament bridge, sometimes for money. She had a reputation as a card shark. But with all these activities, her real interest was fishing. After my family moved to northern Minnesota, she came to visit for a month or more each summer and spent most of the time fishing. The other 11 months she talked fishing and planned her next trip.

Mom never weighed more than 100 pounds and she had arms like toothpicks, but she was tough as barbed wire. In later years, when she arrived for her summer's angling, she would offer the same complaint: "You know I am getting old and my wrists are not as strong as they used to be. If I happen to get a good-sized fish on the line, you will probably have to land it."

"Sure, Mom."

She loved fishing for walleyes and bass with a bobber and leeches. First time out, when the bobber ducked under, she would whisper hoarsely: "I've got a bite."

"O.K., set the hook."

She would carefully reel up until the line was tight, set her jaw, and whip the rod tip back in a sharp arc. Then she alternately reeled and reefed on the rod, horsing the fish right to the boat.

"Gee, Mom, don't rip his head off," I would caution.

"Don't want him to get loose, do we?" she snapped through clenched teeth. So much for her weak wrists.

We took a number of canoe trips into the Boundary Waters and up into Quetico Provincial Park. Once, riding the small riffle from Ensign Lake down into Splash Lake, we paused for a moment where the current eddies around a rock-bound pool. It had been a relatively poor day for fishing, and Mom commented occasionally on our lack of success. "Think there might be any fish in this pool?" she inquired with little enthusiasm.

"It's about time to quit for supper, but we can give it a try," I answered. With that, she cast out her line and squinted at her red and white bobber. With nothing better to do, I lashed the canoe to a sapling, slid out, and climbed the bank for a better look. What I saw took my breath away. Where the July sun slanted into the clear, tea-tinted water, two dozen thick brownish bass shifted back and forth in the current, a good thirty feet from where her bobber floated.

"Reel up, Mom," I commanded, "and cast your line farther upstream, right at the edge of the current."

With a decided lack of enthusiasm, she followed my directions. From above I watched her bait float down to where the school of bass drifted. "Watch out! You're gonna get a bite," I announced as one of the fish shot forward with powerful thrusts of his broad caudal fin. Her bobber dove under, she hauled back, and three pounds of raging smallmouth blew up in a glorious cascade of foam.

"How . . . did . . . you . . . know . . . I . . . was . . . going . . . to . . . get . . . a . . . bite?" Mom gasped, cranking desperately on her reel. She had no idea I was watching the fish.

"Lucky guess." I slid down the bank, netted her fish, impaled it on the stringer, jabbed a fresh crawler on her hook, then scrambled back to my observation point.

The bass had moved a few yards downstream and were now in quiet water, closer to the canoe. "Cast in the slack water, right in front of you," I said.

"How about back up in the current?" From where she was sitting, she could see only shoreline reflections on the surface.

"No . . . in the still water in front of the canoe."

She dutifully cast, and again I watched with fascination as her bait drifted toward the bass school. A second smallmouth, much smaller, darted forward. "You're gonna get another bite," I warned.

The bobber dove, Mom set the hook, and the scenario was repeated. This one was hardly a foot long, and we released it. But by the time the bass in the pool caught on and refused to strike any more, we had five heavy fish on the stringer and paddled toward home in triumph.

I never did tell her how I observed those fish from overhead while she could see nothing at the water level. Many times thereafter she would relate to her friends about the time we had the canoe tied up at the edge of the pool and I pointed to where I thought she should cast.

"It was just uncanny," she would say. "He seemed to know exactly where those bass were hiding, how big each one was, and exactly when it was going to bite."

Of course I did. From up on the bank I could see every last one of them.

On Mom's hundredth birthday, she was honored as the only eighty-year volunteer in the history of the city hospital. She was also guest of honor at a luncheon honoring her as the only living graduate from the first class of our local community college in 1914.

For her centenary, my sister and I rented a spacious hall and held an open house, which was attended by more than three hundred friends of all ages. Mom seated herself at a table near the doorway, where she functioned as sort of a one-person receiving line, making sure she missed no one. As I scurried back and forth carrying trays of sandwiches, cakes, and cups of punch, I happened to pass near the doorway as a bevy of college-age young ladies stopped to offer their congratulations.

"Oh, Mrs. Cary," one bright-eyed youngster gushed. "I bet when you look around at the world now, you long for the good old days."

Mom glanced up sharply, "Young lady, when I was young we had teams of men with brooms and shovels clearing horse manure off the streets; there was no such thing as indoor plumbing, and in the winter time we had to hike to the toilet through snow and ice to a little shed in the backyard. If you want the good old days you are welcome to them. I'll take things just like they are right now."

Entertaining Immunity

It was probably the night that the Beaver Patrol of Scout Troop 48 camped in a patch of poison ivy that I discovered my immunity. The entire patrol of twelve-year-olds broke out with rashes and blisters, except me. Poison ivy was common where I grew up . . . along the streams we fished, and in farm fields and woodlands. In time, my growing reputation of having immunity to poison ivy not only was a source of personal satisfaction, but also provided a modest cash income. People paid me to pull up poison ivy plants around their summer cottages, yards, and gardens.

Later, when married, with two young daughters being initiated into the world of camping, I felt it high time to educate them as to the prevalence of noxious plants. I accepted it as one of the responsibilities of fatherhood. Thus, when once we camped near a patch of poison ivy, I went over and plucked some specimens, bringing them back to camp for the kids to inspect, but not touch. In some detail I explained how the poison worked and how to readily identify the three-leaf clusters. And warned the youngsters to avoid contact at all costs.

"How come you are handling it, Daddy?" our youngest inquired.

"Because Daddy has an unusual tolerance to poison ivy. Daddy is immune, but very few people are. Don't you kids touch it!"

Two days after we came home from the camping trip I developed a case of hives. No doubt, I surmised, from eating too many strawberries. Since it didn't seem to be clearing up, I visited Doc Bender at the clinic.

"Got a case of hives," I informed the doctor. "Got anything for hives?"

"Uh huh," Doc said, inspecting my rash and blisters. "Where'd you get into the poison ivy?"

"No, Doc, it's hives. I'm immune to poison ivy. Always have been."

Doc gave me an amused look. "There isn't any immunity. Some people are more tolerant than others, but anyone can get it when conditions are right."

Doc sent me to Krebs Drug Store with a prescription, and I went home to apply the ointment to my afflicted parts. "What did the doctor say?" my wife inquired.

"He gave me some medicine for my hives."

Lil grabbed the jar of ointment and read the label. "Hah! This says it is for poison ivy."

There were snorts, giggles, snickers, and even outright whoops of laughter that convulsed the whole family.

Over the years, I found that fathers not only have the responsibility to warn and protect children from hazards such as poison ivy, but also to provide entertainment from time to time. Even now, some fifty years later, a mention of "Daddy's immunity" is cause for considerable hilarity.

The Sheer
Wonder of Autumn

The sheer wonder of it all.

How fortunate to be blessed with eyes to see the changing forest patterns and to have those eyes connected by nerve impulses to the mind that can comprehend it all. From the first September splashes of yellow in the birches, through the blazing red and orange of October, the northern world has moved into more muted grey, russet, grey-green, tan, and gold tints of early November.

It is an annual event, this changing from summer through fall to winter, but it is just as awesome this year as it was last year, and it will be awesome again next year. Sometimes one wonders about the mass of humanity so engrossed with artificial stimulation provided on television that the outdoor autumn spectacle, perhaps, is overlooked. The political war rages over a state-funded stadium to house our professional athletic teams, civilization's equivalent of the Roman gladiatorial contests, where roaring crowds gather, for a price, to scream at our football heroes in plastic helmets and massive padding as they smash into one another or to watch a

baseball frenzy where a pitcher hurls a missile in the vicinity of a batter who waves a hickory cudgel not far removed from the war clubs once used to split an opponent's skull. At least professional sports are usually less sanguinary than in ancient times, although perhaps not less costly.

But what an incredible spectacle lies down any woodland path, totally free, where one may simply walk at leisure and absorb the ever-changing scene. Not only are the settings being constantly replaced on the forest stage, but the actors are continually moving on and off.

Sit for a moment on the rough bole of a blown-down pine, and a Canada jay or two will appear on cue, softly, whooshing in, eyes bright with expectation, hoping the human intruder will pitch out a few crumbs from a trailside snack. A black-capped chickadee alights on an adjacent dogwood, head cocked to one side, inspecting this two-legged woodland visitor at close range.

Somewhere out of sight, a pileated woodpecker hammers on a dead popple. Although it's not visible, the imagination can picture a flurry of flying wood chips as the gaunt driller intently probes for insect larvae.

On the move again, the hiking trail leads downhill to a beaver pond created by toothy engineers, whose presence is evident from fresh alder and birch limbs jammed into the mud. Protruding green and yellow leaves create a ragged bouquet above the pond surface. From behind a screen of flooded timber comes the guttural rasp of a black duck intently skimming pondweed from the surface.

A pair of ravens, eyes focused on a wolf kill at some distance, sail past overhead, sunlight glinting off their glistening black plumage. In soft croaks, they converse in flight, anticipating a venison luncheon on leftovers abandoned by gray canine hunters.

The sun leans lower toward the west, and the light bathes the trees with a soft orange glow, in contrast to lengthening bluish shadows. The silence is marred by faint beaver pond creaks and groans, the ice-cover orchestra tuning up. In a night or two, it will begin its winter concert in serious fashion, shrieking and booming as the ice thickens and finally encases the lake surface until spring.

It is a time of year with so much happening. The backdrop ever-changing as the seasonal scene shifts. Over all, the sounds and scents of fall. A few days and it will all be over. The final white curtain will descend, and the entire woodland theater becomes muffled in a white blanket of insulation that assures plant life and the tiny creatures of the forest floor a measure of protection against coming frigid temperatures. Yet one is aware that, inevitably, a spring sun will again open another season of summer theater; the actors gone south for the winter will return with a new production.

In the meantime, however, there is autumn to savor.

Tale of a Cat

Dick Hall tells a story about this family with a large, rather old, black and white cat. The family was leaving for the weekend, and a few days before they were going, they asked their next-door neighbor to check on the cat, make sure it had food and water. On Friday, the neighbor remembered the family had left and was preparing to go over and check on the cat when he was horrified to see his own dog, a rather large and surly beast, come home dragging that same cat by the neck, very bedraggled and very dead. Anticipating big problems when the family returned, he decided to clean up the cat and put it back on the family's porch so they would think it might have died of natural causes instead of being killed by the dog. Thereupon he washed all the dirt out of the cat's fur, dried it carefully with a hair blower, and placed it on the family's porch. And he kept his own dog locked up indoors. Sunday morning, the family came home, drove in the driveway, got out of the car, and recoiled with horror upon seeing the dead cat. Within seconds they were at the neighbor's house. "Guess what happened when we were gone?" the wild-eyed father announced in a shaken voice.

"Your cat died," the neighbor said.

"No, not just that. We forgot to tell you, but our cat died the day before we left, and we buried it in the back yard," he said in a terror-stricken voice. "But when we got back the dead cat had somehow gotten out of the grave, got all cleaned up, and was lying on our front porch."

There's Big Money in Wolf Fur

(Especially If It's Walking Around)

Up to 1965, wolves were worth thirty-five dollars each to the State of Minnesota. That was the bounty fee the Department of Natural Resources paid trappers or hunters for dead wolves. The rationale was that if trappers were paid to wipe out wolves, wild game such as deer would become much more abundant. Proponents envisioned a buck deer standing behind every tree. The wolf, as we were taught from childhood, was a vicious marauder that would not only kill and eat every Bambi in the woods, but might even dine on Little Red Riding Hood's grandmother. Great theater, but not much fact.

In 1965, after years of research, wildlife managers persuaded the Minnesota Legislature to dump the bounty. Cold, hard fact showed that the deer population depended on food and weather. Food was supplied essentially by new growth of hardwoods such as popple, birch, maple, and other browse, usually following timber cutting. Weather patterns indicated that about every eight to

ten years, a severe winter or two, with deep snow and bitter cold, would smack the northern deer population down, and it would take several years to recover. Wolf populations fluctuated right along with the deer. Since the bounty had little relationship to either browse or weather, why waste money on it?

There was a bitter fight in the legislature, but the wolf bounty was laid to rest. Doomsayers predicted the deer would be quickly decimated. It didn't happen. Deer populations continued at peak levels from 1969 though 1971, when a couple of severe winters cracked deer numbers down sharply. The wolf population took a nosedive, too. By 1974, timber wolves were on the federal "endangered species" list, warranting total protection. To be quite accurate, they were endangered in the lower forty-eight states, not exactly as a species, since there was a rather healthy population of wolves ranging over most of neighboring Canada and in Alaska. However, protection from hunting and trapping in Minnesota gave wolves the opportunity to increase in numbers as the deer population recovered, as it had about every eight to ten years. Over time, both deer and wolves increased. Wolves spread into other parts of Minnesota and got a foothold in Wisconsin and Michigan.

The winter of 1996–97 was another hard one on deer, but not as drastic. By 1998, the deer population was on the upswing. So were wolf numbers. Federal trappers took over 200 livestock-raiding wolves in 1998. Biologists believe another 200 died of natural causes. The Minnesota population was estimated at 2,400 animals, compared with 1965, when there were perhaps 1,200 wolves, and 190 bountied for $6,650. Live wolves now bring in more than $1 million annually to the city of Ely. In 1993, the International Wolf Center opened its doors, six thousand square feet of unique exhibits assembled through the Science Museum of Minnesota. Some one hundred thousand visitors each year view the superb displays, featuring an indoor rotunda where taxidermists have created a lifelike pack of twelve wolves in natural poses. Circling this are individual sections depicting the interaction of wolves with humans.

In addition, there is a captive pack of four live wolves in a small woods on the premises. Visitors may watch the pack from within a glassed-in viewing room while technicians go into the outdoor pen, engage in play with adult wolves, and feed them. Thousands of parents, grandparents, and youngsters who may never see a wolf in the wild may view these live wolves eye to eye through the glass barrier. Visitors say there is something about looking into the bold, yellow, nonblinking eyes that evokes a feeling of awe not associated with any other species.

Where we live, on the rim of the Boundary Waters Wilderness, wolves are familiar neighbors. We not only hear their hunting cries at night but often see them in daylight crossing roads, traveling up lake ice, or even coming through the yard.

One frosty, moonlit winter night in 1992, I stepped outside the cabin to gather a wheelbarrow of firewood. Our old cocker/ poodle cross, Nuts of Neverhunt, insisted on accompanying me to the woodshed in the backyard. As we crunched across the hard-packed snow, we were stopped by a low moan from the woods beyond the driveway, then an awful-throated howl. Nuts let out a muffled shriek and bolted for the back door. I tossed some wood chunks into the wheelbarrow and pushed it to the back steps and opened the door. Nuts shot past my legs, cut into the bedroom, and dove headfirst under the bed.

My wife gave me a quizzical look. "Couple of wolves outside," I explained. "Let's go out on the front porch and give them a call."

Wolves are quick to answer a howl, even one emitted by a human if the call is reasonably authentic. I sent a howl toward the

woods and immediately got an answer from behind the wood-shed. But then, almost beneath our feet, came a series of loud cries. Across the front yard in the moonlight were four dark blue shadows of four more wolves. For perhaps ten minutes we kept up the performance, howling and getting answers from a total of six wolves that circled the house, never more than fifty feet away. Then they suddenly vanished, and the woods went silent.

What does something like this mean? I have no idea. I only know that there is something in our heritage, some incomprehensible link between man and wolf left from the mists of time. Wild canines were the first mammals "tamed" by humans and used for hunting, herding, and protection. Significantly, American Indians have wolf clans in every tribe. They identify with the wolf as a brother. Those of us with immigrant European backgrounds have never reached that level, but we have come a long way from the three little pigs and the big bad wolf.

Sometimes We Go on Foot

The snow on Lake One lay white and smooth, broken only by tracks of moose, deer, wolves, otter, mink, and marten. There had been a few cars parked at the Lake One landing and boot prints to the shoreline, but no one had ventured out on the snow-crusted ice. Maybe afraid the ice was not safe, a reasonable assessment considering the kind of winter we are having.

However, the lure of the deep forest, the attraction of "what's around the next bend" was too strong to resist. Procuring a fifteen-foot pole and locking it under my right arm, I took off across the lake, followed by my wife, Edith. See, Edie weighs only 98 pounds, the rationale being that if my 170 pounds could make it across without cracking through, Edie should certainly have safe passage. The pole under the arm simply ensured that if I did break through, I would go underwater only to my chest and have a reasonable chance of crawling back out on the ice.

There were some air holes, unfrozen spots to be avoided, and some slush pockets, but these we skirted and crossed to the far side of Lake One, then followed the shoreline. If we broke through

along shore, we reasoned, we would only go into the water knee-deep or so, not particularly dangerous.

Like all the other days we have had in the past month, the day was unseasonably warm . . . in the upper 20s, the wind little more than a whisper. At the far end of Lake One we crossed a portage trail and came out on the Kawishiwi River, which was a mix of snow-covered ice in the quiet stretches and flowing open water at the riffles. Here we paid particular attention to the ice, traveling on it only tight against shore and sometimes detouring onto the snow-crusted shoreline rocks. The only tracks, other than our own, were those of otter and mink, which meandered in and out of the flowing water, tracks hugging the shore where thin ice was apparent, going over the rocks where there was open water. At one point Edie raised a mitten and pointed upwind. Her sharp hearing had detected the distant moaning cry of a coursing wolf pack.

The winter scene was breathtaking . . . sky cloudless, a deep cobalt backdrop to the green pines and balsams, the slanting winter sun reflecting orange on reaching fingers of leafless aspen.

It was Dorothy Molter who used to say, "People come up here saying they seek solitude . . . I tell them to take off and go hiking inland . . . they'll find more solitude than they know what to do with."

Certainly Edie and I were surrounded by solitude. Over several decades, Christmas travel has been done on snowmobiles, skis, and snowshoes, but this was the only time I could recall simply hiking in mukluks. The snow was not deep enough for snowshoes, and while skis might have worked, the boots were less of a problem on the portages.

Back in the shelter of some jack pines we built a fire, hunkered on a sun-warmed log, and roasted hot dogs. Like kids on a picnic. And we had a couple of plastic bottles of Coke from the packsack to drink (plastic for environmental correctness).

As the December sun slid on its low horizontal orbit toward the west, we backtracked to the public landing, walking through strips of golden snow interspersed with contrasting long blue shadows cast by shoreline pines. All this and not a soul around. Not even a track to indicate anyone else had been on the lake.

It's an incredible country we live in up here, with hundreds of miles of snow-crusted trails. All one needs is a pair of boots and the inclination to use them.

Speckled Trophies of Tiny Brooks

There are, in the vicinity of Isabella, Minnesota, a number of icy-cold little streams that meander northward through dense stands of jack pine, birch, and aspen. These brooks are quite unlike the brawling, boulder-strewn rivers such as the Cascade, Temperance, Baptism, Manitou, Split Rock, Gooseberry, and others of prominence that crash south in thundering froth from the Laurentian Divide to Lake Superior.

By contrast, the small, north-flowing streams, including the Mitawan, Arrowhead, Dumbbell, Inga, Jack, Little Isabella, and Scott, for the most part slide unobtrusively through bog and brush and quietly but resolutely migrate towards the Arctic Ocean.

The one thing all these streams have in common is trout; but the north-flowing brooks contain only scarlet-finned, olive-backed, red-spotted natives untainted by the technology of artificial hatcheries.

For sure, these fish are considerably smaller than the heavyweight rainbows, browns, and specks of the larger rivers, but they are feisty little bantamweights, and their habitat is much more hospitable toward elderly legs and stiff kneecaps than the larger streams.

It is to these user-friendly streams that we ancients migrate in June, less intent upon a trophy than perchance a few tasty eight- or nine-inchers for the pan.

My favorite stretch is adjacent to and north of Highway 1 and Forest Road 172. This is all Superior National Forest, and a visitor is not plagued with "No Trespassing" signs or other impediments of civilization. But it is also very wild country, where travel is often by way of moose trails, and it behooves the trout seeker to carry a good map, a compass, and a knowledge of how to use both.

These streams are not grand, glamorous torrents such as portrayed in the film *A River Runs through It*. They are narrow and overhung with growth, and the speckled residents lie beneath grassy cutbanks, among root thickets and below brushy blowdowns—places beyond reach of the traditional fly-caster no matter how elevated his level of skill. However, a persistent disciple of live bait, with suitable craftiness, may here acquire the essentials for a trout luncheon.

Careful strategy is required because the streams are so tiny and brushy that one must plot a stealthy approach so as not to alarm the aquatic dwellers. A worm, impaled on perhaps a size 10 or 12 hook, is the accepted fare, carefully eased through an opening in the overhang and allowed to drift whither the current may decree 'neath undercut banks and into shadowy pools. Done right, the drift is rewarded with a light tap, then a steady tug as the trout heads for cover.

The ensuing battle is usually furious but, of necessity, brief. If the fish is allowed some headway, it will immediately dive into tree roots or some other unseen hazard. The angler must concentrate on stripping in line at a furious rate, bringing the fish thrashing and crashing to the shore, over the bank, and to hand where it

can be admired, thumped solidly behind the ears, and deposited into a willow creel.

By prearranged agreement, our angling entourage, usually of three or four trout prospectors, will meet at a noon rendezvous where a small fire is kindled, a pot of tea water set to sizzling, and our morning's catch dredged in flour and then rendered golden brown in hot butter. When it's served up with a slice of fresh lemon, the pan drippings carefully applied to our Swedish limpa bread, we stretch out, backs to tree trunks, and dine in utter contentment. At length, with the trout satisfactorily consumed, we refill our cups and perhaps finish off with a ripe apple or peach. Or better yet, a few handfuls of wild strawberries.

Quite likely, as dragonflies drift lightly overhead, we draw from memory trips past, yarns of quests on other streams at other times, forays to distant waters.

Stories pour forth of trout taken in sunshine and in rain, confrontations with moose, deer, and otter and endless hordes of pesky, winged marauders. Stories of hilarity, stories of sadness. Stories of anglers we knew over more than half a century who are no longer with us, who have made the long portage to that mist-shrouded Trout Country Beyond, where the waters are forever clear and a warm wind gently stirs the fragrance from lacy pine boughs. And where, we pray, we may all someday gather again by the fire, compare notes, and raise our cups in salute to all of the trout we have known, large and small—past, present, and future—and to those remote and wonderful places in which they dwell.

Good Morning, Corvus

His name is Corvus Cristatus. He's a handsome fellow, sometimes pretty noisy. And he is tough enough to survive in the northland all winter. Some people consider him somewhat of a thief, but that is not exactly correct. He merely helps himself to whatever is available.

Most of us know him better by the name "blue jay." Corvus Cristatus is his Latin designation. Now, lest someone get the impression that this writer is well-versed in either Latin or ornithology, it ain't so. The reason why I happen to know the blue jay is called Corvus Cristatus is that there is a big print of the bird from a painting by J. J. Audubon hanging in our bathroom over the commode, and every time I have to go to the bathroom, I can't help but look at it. It is a very nice painting, however, like all of Audubon's work. Somewhat stylized with the artist's distinct touch, but certainly excellent for identifying birds. A lot of us grew up with Audubon bird books and learned whatever we may have absorbed through the artist's renderings.

Ely Echoes

This particular painting by John Audubon shows three blue jays raiding the nest of another bird, drilling its eggs and slurping down the yokes. Blue jays will do this. But who's to call them "thieves?" People eat eggs, too, and you hardly ever see a notation on a menu that says: "Two eggs, any style, with toast and coffee . . . stolen from a chicken somewhere." No sirree. We accept that the eggs we eat were intended for that purpose and have no problem—fried, scrambled, or in an omelet.

The blue jay picks up his breakfast wherever he can and devours the eggs raw. We should not judge him for that. Indeed, in some ways he is like a lot of people, in that while he is swiping eggs he continually aims his bill at every other bird in the woods and screams: "Thief ! Thief!"

Revenge of the Otter

To forestall rumors concerning how my upper lip got smashed last week: the damage was done by an otter. See, my boat is parked on a skid so it can be pushed off into the lake when we are going fishing. Thus it was that last week I was sliding the boat down the skid to the water when suddenly my feet slipped out from underneath me and my face hit the gunwale. Heck of a bang. First, I felt to make sure my front teeth were still in place. They were, but my lip was split wide open and blood was running off my chin. Once that got stanched, I went to look at what caused my feet to slip on the skid. It was a fresh pile of wet otter doo-doo.

Canoe Season

It's canoe season again.

The 1998 canoe season actually got underway two weeks ago, when the ice went off the rivers and local paddlers began dipping blades into the Burntside and Shagawa rivers. Of course, just about all the ice blew off the lakes early last week, so canoes can go anywhere now; however, a week ago there was still ice on most waters. But not on the rivers. And the rivers were where we went.

There is a nice landing on the Burntside River just off the Wolf Lake Road, marked by signs and a parking lot. It was Easter Sunday afternoon, with the temperature hovering at about 65, a warm breeze stirring the spruce trees and a lot of early ducks treading upstream and down. We unloaded the canoes and negotiated the wood-bridge portages to the shore.

Nobody was around. Not a soul. From the tracks in the mud, it looked like maybe a couple of canoes had been on the river days earlier. But nobody this Easter.

Our craft were two Kevlar hulls, eighteen-footers. Andy and Paula Hill in the lead canoe, Edie and I in the second one. That upper part of the river, about a half mile from where it comes out of Burntside Lake, is narrow, with a moderate current curving

over a rock and sand bottom. The current was all the more moderate because of poor winter snow and lack of spring runoff.

Several times we negotiated beaver dams, two built atop small falls. At the bottom of the last portage, we built a small fire on the wet mud and cooked up a package of hot dogs. These we woofed down with pretzels and Pepsi.

Where the river meandered into the flatter country, it spread out and got shallower. Bunches of ducks appeared. First some goldeneye, then mergansers, and lastly numbers of mallards, loudly protesting our invasion.

We passed behind the old Knuutti dairy farm, no longer in operation, and wondered about those earlier days when hardy homesteaders carved out a living furnishing milk for Ely families and cutting tons of marsh hay to keep their cows through the winter.

We passed under a new bridge where a gravel lane angled south from Forest Road 404 to a new riverside development .

At one point, a beaver came out of the bank, swam beneath both canoes, turned about, and went back into the bank den. Muskrat pushups and houses were apparent, but we saw none of those little brown rodents.

On a shallow bar, a school of suckers churned away, indicating that in spite of a few snowbanks still in the woods, spring is going to be a lot earlier than usual. Although cattails and marsh grass were dead brown, a few green shoots showed here and there, and pussy willows were fuzzing out.

It was a long and somewhat uninteresting winter, but it appears that we are going to have a very early and fun-filled spring. Time to think about crappies and sunfish in the shallows. Time to varnish the paddle and get ready for summer.

Time to paddle again.

142

It's a Matter of Patriotic Belief

For many of us, it is really a matter of patriotism. That is, our belief in America, its constitution, its woods, waters, historical heritage, and fish—mainly the fish—require us to solemnly observe Opening Day, which is coming up Saturday, May 15. Many of the nonfishing folk do not understand this. Sometimes not even members of our own families.

There is a misdirected assumption among some nonfishing folk that we are engaged in some form of recreation, that we really enjoy heading forth by boat or canoe to seek a limit of walleyes, northern pike, bass, or trout. Nothing could be farther from the truth. The truth is, we take our civic responsibilities very seriously, our Pledge of Allegiance, and one of these responsibilities is to be on the water, duly armed with rod and reel on Opening Day.

Just how seriously we view this can be determined by the weather. On many Opening Days, there has been ice along the shore, sometimes ice on the boat seats, sleet blowing in, and even snow. Grimly, we put on an extra sweater, zip up our rain jackets,

pick up our tackle, and head out anyway. We believe that strongly in duty to our country.

Not only that, we put our money where our mouths are. Not a single one of us hesitates a moment to spend whatever necessary to support our patriotic fervor. We think nothing of shelling out $50 to $75 for a fishing rod, another $50 to $75 for a reel, and we do not even keep track of lines, lures, and other accoutrements.

In addition, we willingly pay $15 right off the top for a resident fishing license. That is, if we are between the ages of sixteen and sixty-four. And because our governor and state legislators are similarly motivated by patriotism —which they wish to see taught to the state's youth—kids up to age sixteen can engage their devotion to duty by fishing free. And older folk, Veterans of the Fishing Wars (VFW), get a reduced rate of $5.50 for their fishing licenses. Husbands and wives get a special combinted rate of $20.50.

Patriots from other states are really tested as to their steadfastness. We bill them $37 for a single license or $41.50 for the family. It is a tribute to that dedication to the American tradition that thousands of citizens from other states come here each Opening Day to help us observe this important facet of our heritage.

Thus you will find us at sunrise next Saturday, getting our weapons from the car, buckets of ammunition sloshing in Flo-Troll containers, thumping down to the shore in rubber-bottom pacs for the initial assault. A last-minute check is made to determine if life vests are aboard, and then, either by motor or paddle, we head out upon the misty battleground, jaws set with determination to give our all for God, our nation, and the Stars and Stripes.

And if our efforts are rewarded, if we manage to vanquish a few scaly opponents and impale them upon our stringers forthwith, we will be rewarded by a sense of accomplishment. At noon, as we munch soggy rations and scalding coffee, we may well pause for a moment in silent respect for all those veterans who have gone before us into the angling wars and who are no longer among our ranks. But only a moment will we pause, for the war is not over, and there are battles to be won.

With gritting teeth we dip our hands into the ice water, grasp another wriggling minnow, impale it upon the hook, and solemnly cast it out.

Perhaps later that night, with a few trophy fillets browning in the frying pan, we will have time to reflect on the events of the day and how well we measured up to the challenge. Deep down we will all have that satisfactory feeling that we have done what our nation requires of us.

Opening Day. It is our patriotic duty.

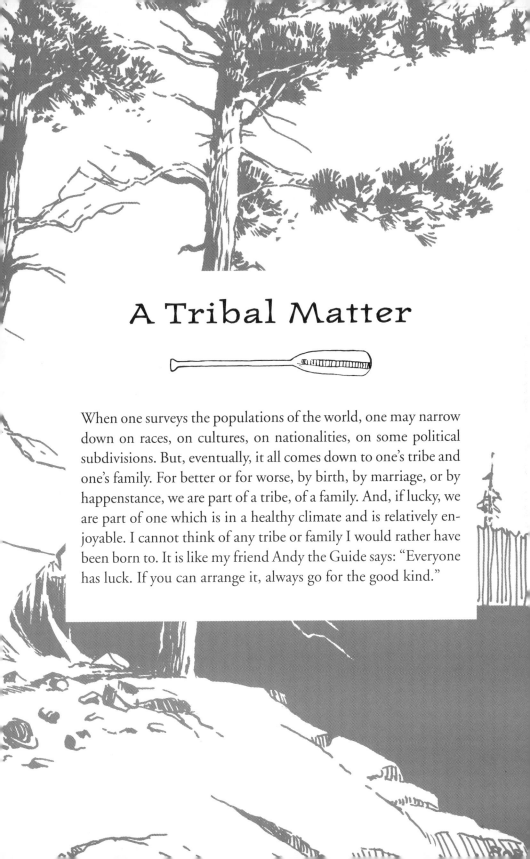

A Tribal Matter

When one surveys the populations of the world, one may narrow down on races, on cultures, on nationalities, on some political subdivisions. But, eventually, it all comes down to one's tribe and one's family. For better or for worse, by birth, by marriage, or by happenstance, we are part of a tribe, of a family. And, if lucky, we are part of one which is in a healthy climate and is relatively enjoyable. I cannot think of any tribe or family I would rather have been born to. It is like my friend Andy the Guide says: "Everyone has luck. If you can arrange it, always go for the good kind."

Honoring a Promise to Tommy Chosa

Colorful. Laconic. Competent. Contrary. Perceptive. All were words to describe Tommy Chosa, last of the old-time Indian guides from Ely.

He was also one of the last people to own private land inside the Boundary Waters Canoe Area—forty acres he had purchased from the U.S. government. That's the same U.S. government that snookered Tommy's Ojibwe ancestors out of the whole area under the Treaty of 1854.

Yet there were still Ojibwe people living at Washington Island, Prairie Portage, and Jackfish Bay of Basswood Lake until that same government decided it was a wilderness and that white men could not abide Indians dwelling in "our" wilderness.

None of this was lost on Tommy, although he tended not to touch the subject and offend the white fishermen who paid him to find them walleyes, a pursuit for which he was eminently qualified.

Tom died two years ago, and his kinfolk buried him on Basswood Lake. But in the years before that, when he sometimes had a day off, he was apt to wander into the *Ely Echo* newspaper office

to sip coffee, talk fishing, and perhaps unload a few items that were on his mind.

It was one of the those warm summer days when he took a couple of sips from his mug, squinted sharply at me, and asked, "Did you see the archaeologists?"

"What archaeologists?" I inquired.

"Three of them . . . came to town from the University of Minnesota."

"Nope . . . didn't come in here. Did they come to see you?"

"Yeah. Wanted to know if I knew the location of the Indian burial grounds on Jackfish Bay."

"Heck, you know that, Tom. They wanted to go up there?"

"Yeah . . . said they would give me three hundred dollars to run them up in my fishing boat."

"Lot of money for a boat ride," I noted. "Did you take them?"

"No-o-o," Tom said slowly. "I told them they didn't have to go that far. I said they could just drive out to the edge of Ely on the east side. They looked puzzled for a minute. Then one of them said: 'You mean the Ely Cemetery?' 'Yeah,' I said. 'Go dig up your people . . . don't dig up mine.' "

When I finally quit laughing, I found Tommy's coal black eyes burrowing straight into mine. "How come," he hissed, "when you die you are just dead; but when an Indian dies he becomes an artifact?"

I looked at my typewriter, at the ceiling, at the floor, and out the front window. "I don't know, Tom," I said softly. "I have lived three quarters of a century and I sometimes don't understand my people . . . what they do and how they think. But I promise that someday I will write about this and perhaps someone more learned than I can come up with some answers."

January Ice
and Snow

The lake ice, which started booming in November, has now thickened and settled into an occasional guttural grunt. Puffs of white vapor drift away with each breath as we squint at the outdoor thermometer. The red line of mercury terminates at 22 below. Dry, hard-packed trail snow creaks beneath sled runners, skis, and mukluks. But the sky is a cloudless, deep cobalt and the sun glints on myriad snow crystals stretching in an unbroken, sequined blanket to the blue-green shoreline rim of spruce and fir.

It is time to go out and see what the trout are about.

As they have for centuries, men, dogs, sleds, skis, and snowshoes trek into the back country, following a primitive urge that reaches back to our fur-clad ancestors, who relished the flavor of fresh-caught winter fish and devised simple but clever means for harvesting them.

True, our tackle is more sophisticated. But the system is the same. We have little more real knowledge about trout beneath the ice than those long-forgotten anglers who chopped holes in the frozen surface and patiently jigged with primitive gear.

Long before the English writer Izaak Walton penned his now-famous treatise *The Compleat Angler* in 1653, men (and a few women) sought finny dwellers of the ice-water world. There is no evidence that Walton ever pursued his prey beneath the ice and he was probably the poorer for it. Certainly his fishing knowledge was one-dimensional, stunted.

For those who pursue it, ice-fishing has a certain attraction all its own. There is the eternal hope that somewhere in the depth beneath one's feet cruise schools of sleek trophies. Patiently, the mittened angler raises and lowers his tackle, alert to that solid tug that indicates a strike.

From the initial impact of the hook set, hot blood begins to course through hands and feet numbed by the cold; perhaps even a trickle of sweat dribbles down the parka-protected neck. The rod throbs and bends, line is taken in, line is stripped out. The monofilament stutter-steps erratically around the hole as the fish lunges against the relentless pressure on his jaw.

With luck, the trout may emerge from the hole in a flurry of ice chips, to land flopping on the snow. No gleaming summer-hooked stream trout eased from the current and into a net has ever outshone a winter prize slapping its broad caudal fin on a snow-packed lake surface.

It's grand ritual . . . and how fortunate we northern dwellers are to participate.

The Night the Aliens Came

"The spaceship was hovering over the trees just to the north of the Fernberg Road between Ely and Wood Lake" was the startling report we printed on the front page of the *Ely Echo* newspaper. The story went on to say it was disc-shaped, silvery, with a row of bright lights all around the outside rim.

The account was accompanied by a slightly blurred but legible photo of the space craft, lights and all, just above a row of popple trees, which appeared like thin, black fingers protruding from the darkness below. Without question, it was one of the most convincing pictures ever taken of an alien spaceship, and it proudly bore the credit line of the Senior Editor. So did the somewhat colorful story describing this invader of the earth's atmosphere.

That this "eyewitness" account would stir the interest of our readers was a foregone conclusion. Hardly had the paper hit the streets and mail boxes when the telephone in the office began to ring. Readers were frantically seeking more details on this strange phenomenon.

To each inquiry, we asked, "Did you read the story?"

The answer was a breathless "Yes!"

"The whole story?"

"What do you mean?"

"The story is continued over on page two. Did you read the final paragraph on page two?"

This was followed by a rustle of paper, a gasp, and some comment to the effect that the Senior Editor was a lying, rotten so-and-so.

The front-page story, of course, was pure fiction. The photo of the alien spaceship was taken in the dark newspaper basement. The "craft" itself consisted of two aluminum pie plates glued together with a short string of tiny Christmas tree lights fastened around the rim. The whole works was suspended from a beam by a black thread, and to give the appearance of a woods, tree branches were stuck in a box so that just the tips would show in the darkness. The "craft" was set in motion with a slight push and as it swung back and forth, a number of photos were taken at various time settings. Out of it all, a couple turned out quite realistic in the photo lab.

Oh, the last paragraph of the story, on page two of our April 1 edition, simply stated "Happy April Fool's Day!"

Most of our readers had a great laugh over it. A few got a trifle upset and said so, to which the Senior Editor replied, "We just wanted to teach you to be just a little skeptical about whatever you may see in print."

A few never did get to page two. A week after the story ran, two quite elderly maiden sisters came into the newspaper and leaned over the front counter, and one whispered, "You know that story you did on the space ship?"

"Yes, what about it?"

"Well, we didn't want to tell our neighbors, but it came across the lake and flew right over our house, just above the tree tops, just as plain as could be." And with that, they scurried out the door.

(The Senior Editor has always wondered if these two old ladies were so terribly taken in that they engaged in self-deception. On the other hand, what if they really did see something?)

Second Time Around

I proposed marriage to Edith Annette Sommer on the first fairway of the Ely Municipal Golf Course. It was November 1997, but we were not playing golf. We were crosscountry skiing. Skiers are aware that the first skiing each winter is likely to be had at the local golf course because it requires a mere three inches of snow over the smooth grass to provide an adequate surface. Both of us are ski racers, and we train regularly.

Indeed, we had been skiing every day for two weeks when I popped the question. And for two months prior to that we had exercised daily on the blacktopped Fernberg Road, using roller skis. In addition, we had more or less canoed together, fished together, and hunted grouse together, and occasionally went to church together. Both widowed after long and very successful marriages, we were somewhat cautious. As senior citizens, we were both aware that one must be quite lucky to experience one good marriage in one's lifetime. But two? There are, unquestionably, some lessons one learns with several decades of marriage, two of which are to develop a strong faith in God and to accept life with a good sense of humor. We were both aware that with our skiing and exercise activities (Edie is a marathon runner), canoeing, fish-

ing, and shooting were considered somewhat eccentric by some segments of the general public, but we were too old and having too much fun to be self-conscious. Our wedding date was set, after some deliberation, for Saturday, February 21, 1998. We picked a Saturday, when our kids would not be at work and the grandchildren would not be in school.

The wedding announcement was placed in the *Ely Echo* newspaper, where I happen to be Senior Editor. It was very similar to all the other wedding announcements that appear regularly. Even the photo. But instead of our current, somewhat timeworn images, we used our college yearbook photos from a half century earlier, quite young and relatively good-looking. Amazingly, half the town skimmed over the notice and didn't recognize it was really us. The other half of the town cracked up.

Obstacles to the wedding began to appear immediately. The Rev. Mike DeArruda, pastor of my church, left on a mission to South America. Edie's was not available. Fortunately, we were friends with the Rev. Elton Brown, a ski racer, and pastor of the Methodist Church at the University of Minnesota, Duluth. Unfortunately, Elton informed us, February 21 was the date of the famed American Birkebeiner Ski Race at Hayward, Wisconsin, and he, as a longtime skier, was signed to compete.

Thinking fast, we suggested that we set the wedding hour for late afternoon, allowing Elton time to finish the thirty-one-mile race and drive from Hayward back to Duluth, change clothes, and meet us at the church. Everything was set, the wedding came off, but not exactly as planned. Since we subsequently received a large number of inquiries concerning the event and our honeymoon in Florida, we chronicled the occurrences and ran them in the newspaper. The following is that story, verbatim.

A Honeymoon of Laughs and Giggles

Most readers of the *Ely Echo* are aware that Senior Editor Jackpine Bob and Edith Annette Sommer were married at 5 P.M., Saturday, February 21, at the University United Methodist Church in Duluth.

Since they returned from the honeymoon, a number of citizens have inquired as to how the honeymoon "went." This requires a rather lengthy explanation, not easy for a seventy-six-year-old groom and a sixty-four-year-old bride. So we have recorded herein some of the highlights to save time and alleviate boredom among *Echo* readers. Chronologically, it went like this:

Feb. 17—Five days prior to the wedding. Edith catches the flu.

Feb. 21—Day of wedding. Bob came down with the flu.

Feb. 21—Pastor Elton Brown, slated to officiate at the wedding, took a bad fall that morning in the Birkebeiner Ski Race at Hayward, Wisconsin, and knocked himself unconscious. He managed to recover and arrive in time to perform the ceremony, but in obvious pain. Edith's daughter-in law, Ann Sommer, sick with flu and two grandsons, Alex and Isak, sick with flu. Son Jay OK. Daughter Annette and son-in law Joe Baltich OK. Bob's daughter Barb and son-in-law, Steve Hall, OK.

Feb. 21—Bride and groom sick with flu at Fitger's Inn, Duluth.

Feb. 22—Groom sicker. Turns into St. Mary's Hospital 24 Hour Emergency Walk-In. Doctor says it is now bronchitis. Prescribes antibiotics.

Feb. 23, 1 P.M—Not so sick. Prepare to fly Duluth to Ft. Lauderdale, Florida, on Northwest Airlines. 3 P.M.—Fog rolls in, flight canceled. Attendant books alternate 6 P.M. flight out of Minneapolis on Continental Airlines to Ft. Lauderdale.

Feb. 23, 3:30 P.M.—Bride and groom race to Minneapolis in Hertz Rent-A-Car, setting new speed record on I-35. Arrive Continental desk five minutes before flight leaves. Skycap named Ron Sterling and Continental attendants rush us through check-in. Last passengers on board. Arrive Houston, connect to Ft. Lauderdale, arrive 1 A.M., Feb. 24. Get Alamo rental car and drive to Airport Ramada, set up by Boundary Waters Travel.

Feb. 24, 7 A.M.—Drive to Key West, check in at Holiday La Concha. Door key does not work. Back down to desk for new key, which does work. Wander uptown to see palm trees, blue ocean, people in shorts.

Feb. 25, 1 A.M.—Groom gets up to go to bathroom, hits foot on bride's suitcase, and breaks second toe on right foot. Develops decided limp.

Feb. 25, noon—Toe feels better. Decide to walk around Key West island, about twelve miles. After six miles, toe is screaming. Become lost in eastern Key West. Meet young Cuban kid on bicycle. Julio explains how to get back to hotel. Thank Julio and offer him a dollar for his courtesy, Julio declines dollar at first, but finally accepts . . . rides off on bike, but comes right back. "Do you have another dollar? I would like to buy a beer for my girlfriend, too," he explains. We provide another dollar.

Feb. 25, 7 P.M.—Back at hotel. Eat supper at Le Artiste Restaurant. Nice but pricey.

Feb. 26—Drive to Lower Matecumbe Key to Boy Scout High Adventure Sea Base for meeting with members of advisory committee, Boy Scout Canoe Base, Ely. Realize Northwest flight tickets from Ft. Lauderdale to Washington, D. C. got picked up by Continental attendant at Minneapolis. Call Northwest 800 number to explain dilemma. Voice says to call travel agent.

Feb. 27, 9 A.M.–noon—Meetings on high adventure programs. Phoned travel agent at Ely. They had booked motels and rental car but not flights. Suggest calling Northwest again. Wives take walk and go see sights on Keys. Evening supper is seafood luau on beach. Lobster, crab, shrimp, fish. Standing in buffet line, several delegates inquire as to limp. Groom explains how he broke his toe. Jostling in buffet line causes bride to take half step backward. Her heel comes down solidly on groom's broken toe. Rest of evening spent on sofa with foot elevated and icepack on toe. Call Northeast 800 number about ticket to Washington, D. C. Voice on other end says, "We have you on the computer. It's OK Just go to the counter at Ft. Lauderdale and check in for flight."

Feb. 28—More Scout meetings in a.m. Scenic boat ride on gulf and on ocean in afternoon. Drive to Ft. Lauderdale. Check in 7 P.M. at Airport Ramada. Find room not cleaned, bed not made. Back to motel office. Girl arrives to inspect room. We show her unmade bed and wet towels on bathroom floor. "What's the problem?" she asks.

Finally get clean sheets and towels. Take Ramada courtesy car to airport to check on missing tickets to Washington, D.C. Arrive 8:15 P.M. to find ticket window shut down. Also coffee shop. Back to Ramada for night.

Feb. 28, 5 A.M.—Up early, return car to Alamo. Take courtesy bus to airport and go to Northwest counter as it opens. Attendant finds us on computer, asks for our tickets. We explain ticket problem via Continental. Attendant says no ticket, no flight.

"Your guy at the 800 number said we were booked on this flight and it would be OK," we pointed out. Attendant does more things with his computer. Says, "Oh, you are on electronic tickets." Issues boarding passes. We board flight for Washington, D.C.

Arrive Dulles Airport—Edith's sister Rosemary and brother-in-law Carl Blechschmidt meet us, drive us to Best Western in Potomac, Maryland. Get nice room but discover somebody else's luggage and clothes in room. Back down to desk. Attendant

baffled, but assigns us another room, which, luckily, is not occupied. Have fabulous chicken dinner at Rosemary's. Nervous groom meets Edith's mother, Helen Kennedy, and assorted in-laws. All very friendly people.

March 1—Brother-in-law Carl drives us to Subaru dealership managed by Edith's niece Annette's husband, Mark Painter. Edith explains there are a lot of people named Annette in her family. Acquire nifty new Subaru. Drive to Gettysburg Battlefield National Park with Rosemary and Carl, tour battlefield. Back to Potomac for night.

March 2—Off early morning for drive back home in new Subaru. Get lost on Pennsylvania Turnpike and wind up driving back toward Washington, D. C. Take twenty-five miles to get off turnpike and turned around.

March 2, 8 P.M.—Still on turnpike in middle of driving blizzard. Fuel light comes on, indicating car is out of gas. Manage to get to Sandusky, Ohio, on fumes. Find Sunoco gas station. Cannot get gas because station is fully automated taking only Sunoco credit cards. Drive to Amoco up road and get gas tank filled.

Check in at Hampton Inn. Park car, bring in luggage, get to room. No card key. Walk to parking lot and find card key on ground next to parked car. Spend night at Hampton Inn. Flu better. Toe better.

March 3 to 6—Drive to Joliet, Illinois, visit with mother, sister Joyce, brother-in law Howie Scheidt. Stay three nights with Bob and Shirley Hamilton, who own summer home at Ely. Visit cousin Bill Paull and wife, Pat, in Aurora, Illinois

March 7—Drive to Wilmette to meet friends Carl and Betty Raglin. Get lost in Chicago looking for Wilmette and arrive one and a half hours late for lunch.

March 7, 3 P.M.—Drive to Black River Falls for overnight.

March 8—Drive to Minneapolis, book into Holiday Inn for night. Notice climate is a lot colder than on Florida Keys.

March 9—Drive to Duluth to visit daughter, Barb, and then back to Ely.

March 10—Back on job at *Echo,* between fits of laughter, trying to fit together pieces for this chronicle. Toe nearly healed up. Flu symptoms almost gone. Things are looking up.

Wesley Ottertail

Tucked way in the shelter of Wilkins Bay, on the northeast side of huge Lac La Croix, is Zup's Fishing Resort and Canoe Outfitters. It was here, the summer of our first year of marriage, that Edith and I landed aboard one of Jay Handberg's Canadian Beaver floatplanes, taxied up to the dock, and disembarked. Over several decades, my first wife, Lil, and I had outfitted numerous canoe trips into Ontario's Quetico Provincial Park through Zup's, and it was my intent to introduce Edie to the scenic western portion of the park, containing Rebecca Falls, Curtain Falls, stands of towering white pines, and lakes teeming with bass and walleyes.

At Zup's we picked up our Ontario fishing licenses and camping permit, packed our duffle and trail food, and loaded our canoe and gear onto Zup's towboat. This roomy, outboard-powered launch headed out from the dock toward the portage into McAree Lake, twenty-five miles east. At the helm was veteran driver Wesley Ottertail, guide from the Ojibwe First Nation and a lifelong resident of the native village on the Neguagon Indian Reserve. Dark of hair and complexion, with nearly coal black eyes, Wes rarely, if ever, expressed any emotion. Indeed, other than a few grunts, he seldom made any attempt to communicate.

Anxious to show Edie a good time on our first canoe trip together, I tried to engage Wesley in conversation, but to no avail. An attempt to introduce Edie to Wes did not elicit even a nod of recognition from our boat driver. And when I pointed out that at my age of seventy-seven and Edie's of sixty-five, we two weather-lined voyageurs were probably somewhat of a rarity on wilderness canoe trails, Wesley shrugged. A half hour later, at the McAree portage, we unloaded our canoe and duffle and bid Wes a hearty good-bye, to which he nodded without emotion and left.

We had a great canoe trip, and it was not until we were back home several weeks later that we encountered a couple from Ely who had outfitted through Zup's two days after we had. By accident, they were following the same route we took, including the long towboat ride up Lac La Croix with the ever-silent Wesley. Like us, our friends attempted to get a conversation going, but with little success. At length, one inquired, "Did Cary come through here recently?"

Wesley nodded slightly in the affirmative.

"When?"

Wes raised two fingers: "Two days ago."

"Where was he going?"

Wes aimed a finger toward the east end of the lake.

Running out of something to say, my friend volunteered, "Say, Wes, did you meet Cary's new wife?"

Wes turned slowly and stared at my friend. "She didn't look so new to me," he said.

Which was no doubt the truth, and also probably the longest statement any of us have heard Wesley utter in more than three decades.

Veteran's Fishing Trip

It was colder than the dickens, that first spring the Ely VFW and American Legion held the Veteran's Fishing Weekend at the new Veterans' on the Lake resort facility. The ice had been off Fall Lake for just a few days, and there were skeins of snow in the air. About fifty patients and staff from the St. Cloud VA Hospital were on hand for Opening Day, and about forty guides and other volunteers, including the Women's Auxiliaries, were taking care to see the patients had a good time. Well, as good as you can with that kind of weather.

It was not easy to leave the cozy warmth of the lodge, brush snow off the boat seats, and motor up Fall Lake. Because ice-out had been so late, the most experienced guides, like Soapy Hedloff, asserted that if there were any fish biting they would be at the outlet of the Fall Lake Power Dam. And that's where everyone headed.

Each boat had a guide and two or three patients, except the big pontoon boat. Vietnam veteran Bob Niskala was at the wheel, WWII veteran "Jake" Jacobsen handled the anchor in the bow,

166

and I was amidships to help keep hooks baited and lines untangled among the six patients on board.

When we arrived at the Power Dam, about thirty boats were already clustered there, anchored in the currents. It was quickly apparent that very few fish were being caught, with one exception. Guide Billy Mills had somehow managed to anchor in a hot spot, right over a school of fish. The two patients in his boat were regularly hauling in walleyes, which Billy duly netted and placed on the stringer.

Ex-Marine Soapy Hedloff, being of a competitive nature, did not accept this easily. Soapy usually came in with the best catch, but this day was not going well. Hedloff's boat was experiencing no luck at all. Seeing what Mills was doing, Soapy tried to thread his boat through the flotilla and get closer, but there were too many other craft in the way.

At 11:30 A.M., somebody hollered, "Lunchtime!" and everyone pulled up their anchors to head for the resort. All except Soapy. The moment Billy Mills got underway, Soapy motored over and dropped his anchor in the exact spot where Mills had been fishing. Obviously, Soapy was not going in for lunch.

After we had sandwiches and coffee at the lodge, about half the original flotilla went back up to the Power Dam. The other guides and patients opted to stay indoors by the fireplace, where there were hot drinks and snacks.

Again, our cumbersome pontoon boat was the last to arrive at the current below the Power Dam. Niskala was at the wheel again, Jake with the anchor in the bow, and me amidships. "Look at that son of a gun." Jake pointed at Hedloff's boat. "Still anchored right where Billy Mills was fishing."

"I see him," Niskala said grimly.

At no-wake speed we threaded our way through the throng of boats, zigzagging toward Soapy. When were about thirty feet away,

Soapy stood up and motioned us not to come any closer. Niskala stayed right on course.

"Hey, you guys!" Soapy yelled. "You're getting too close!"

Niskala kept the bow aimed at Soapy's craft, Jake standing poised on the bow holding the big iron anchor by its rope. Slowly the gap between the boats narrowed to fifteen feet, then ten. "Look out!" Soapy howled in dismay.

With a resounding bang the twin pontoons smacked into the side of Soapy's boat, knocking him off his feet. He scrambled back up, letting fly a colorful stream of profanity. At that point, Jake leaned over and dropped our anchor with a loud clang directly inside Soapy's boat.

With a howl of rage, Soapy shook his fist at Jake. "What the heck do you think you're doing?"

Jake calmly tied off the anchor rope. "Isn't this where they're biting?" he asked coolly.

Red-faced with fury, Soapy sputtered and fumed, threw our anchor over the side, pulled in his own, started up his motor, and roared down the lake toward the resort. The disabled vets in our pontoon boat looked about as stunned as I was; but then everybody laughed, joined by the other guides and patients in the other boats. That evening after supper, Billy Mills won the honorary award for being the best guide of the day. Soapy didn't even wait around. Still angry, he left before supper. If I remember right, Bob Niskala and Jake won the Sportsmanship Award.

There's Nothing Wrong with a Fish Dinner

The sun was coming up somewhere, but it was not visible except for a pale luminescence appearing above a curtain of blue-gray mist ghosting off the black surface of Moose Lake. Off in the distance, the quavering cry of a solitary loon mourned the passing of summer.

Lying on the grass, hull side up, the canoe wore a thin coating of white frost. It was the second day of fall, the season the Ojibwe people call Waatebagaa, the leaves-turning moon.

Our destination lay two portages up. Really, one portage and one drag-through, upstream through a riffle we can sometimes paddle in the spring. But now it was nearly dry, with barely two inches of water trickling over the rocks. A family of dam-building beavers had taken matters into their own hands, probably determining that the lake was vanishing in the dry spell. Of course, the lake couldn't get much lower, but the beavers didn't know that. So they were constructing a dam in the spillway from the lake. Also,

none of them had figured out that next spring when the ice goes out, the dam would wash downstream with a rush and a roar. Their consideration right now was simply to plug the leak out of the lake, and they were doing a good job with branches, mud, and rocks.

My neighbor Bob Hamilton and I simply slid the canoe over the dam and kept going. We were essentially on a food safari. That is, we were seeking some walleye fillets for a supper entree. In the minnow bucket were two dozen rainbow chubs. On our spin rods were eighth-ounce orange jigs. Beyond the beaver dam, we eased onto a sunken bar to engage in hostilities. The sun was out now, reflecting off the water with mirror brilliance. A few wisps of mist were still curling off the sheltered bays, but the sky overhead was cloudless, deep blue.

Shoreline aspen were turning yellow. Maples splashed orange and red against a backdrop of dark green spruce and fir. Exposed rock ledges were blanketed with reddish-purple sumac. High overhead, wedges of Canada geese winged their way across the sky, drifting not only south, but east and west, as though aimlessly seeking out fields for feeding. Of course their journey is far from aimless, and they know exactly where they are going, but from those of us earthbound, they simply appeared to be drifting.

Oh, the walleyes? Between a few strikes by northern pike that clipped off our jigs and minnows, we managed a half dozen "eaters," golden-sided fish in the one-pound to three-pound class. Shirley Hamilton fried three fish—six fillets—for supper. A veritable feast, with baked potatoes and salad. These are indeed the golden days of autumn.

Recycling Grouse

Let it be said that we who live out in the woods are up to speed on the environment, particularly recycling. For instance, a ruffed grouse flew through the window of my Cousin Willie's cabin last week. Ka-Boom! Killed it deader than last week's news. "What a shame," said Willie, looking sorrowfully at the colorful bird. "Not so," I replied, "one must have faith that the Lord provideth. He hath provideth a dinner."

Thus it was that the grouse was dressed out, properly cut up, and made part of a wild rice casserole. Waste not, want not, as our pioneer forebears said.

Busy

Flying conservation officer Bob Hodge banked over the south shore of Shagawa Lake, brought the nose of the Cessna 180 around into the west wind, and cut the throttle back. Flaps down, he was descending toward the seaplane base when his sharp eyes picked out a foreign object underwater just offshore. "Gill net," he said half aloud, marked its location, and then glided in for the landing. At the hangar he rang up his fellow officer Bob Jacobsen.

"Jake?"

"Yeah."

"Bob . . . Listen I was just coming in over Shagawa and spotted a gill net in front of Busy Schiltz's place. I think it belongs to Busy."

"Son of a gun," Jake said. "He'll probably be checking the net for walleyes just about dawn tomorrow. We can't just confiscate the net. We'll have to catch him in the act in order to make the case stick."

"Yeah."

Thus it was that the two veteran conservation officers were concealed in the brush a short distance from Schiltz's cabin, where they could watch the cabin and the area where the net was anchored. It was late fall, bitter cold and drizzly, but the two officers were old hands at patrolling under tough circumstances. Silent, motionless, they waited in the predawn darkness. Busy Schiltz was sort of a north country spirit who lived occasionally on the edge of the law or just over the edge. Like a number of Ely old-timers, he felt that the natural resources such as fish and game were put on earth by Providence for use by those in need. And Busy considered himself in need much of the time. It wasn't that he was a chronic law violator; it was just that when it came to fish and game, he thought the Minnesota fishing and hunting seasons were not always scheduled at the time of greatest need. And state-specified fishing methods, such as use of a single hook and line, were not particularly efficient. Nets were surer, but had the uncomfortable side effect of bringing down the wrath of law enforcement officers on the fisherman's head.

At any rate, Hodge and Jacobsen thought they had set a near-perfect trap for Busy, although the setting was not especially comfortable. As the minutes ticked by, they became wetter and colder, blowing hot breath on their chilled fingers as they waited.

Just as it was getting gray over in the east, a light came on in Busy's cabin. Then smoke began pouring from the stovepipe, indicating a fire had been kindled. At this point, the door opened and Busy stuck his head out. "Bob! Jake!" he called loudly. "Come on in and have some hot coffee."

Mystified at how they had been discovered, they stumbled on stiff legs to the door, entered the warm cabin, and slumped down at the table. Busy served up hot mugs of brew, and as they sipped their steaming coffee, the suspense was getting to them. Finally Hodge asked the big question:

"Busy . . . how the heck did you know we were hiding out there in the bushes?"

"I didn't," Busy grinned. "I yell like that every morning when I get up."

Those with Four Legs, More or Less

Other than receiving Social Security checks, there are not many advantages to being a grandfather. But watching kids discover the out-of-doors may be even better than the checks.

Edie's grandkids from Walker were up for a visit last week, and they wanted to take a hike. At ages seven and three, kids need an adult to accompany them in the woods. And it so happened that Grandpa Bob was available, so off we went on the network of ski and hiking trails on the property adjacent to the Moose Lake Road. Seven-year-old Alex is extremely agile and had no problem keeping up or running ahead. Three-year-old Isak had to double-time his legs to keep up with his older brother, sometimes sprinting, sometimes lagging a hundred feet behind.

As we came over a ridge bisected by an electric power line, four deer jumped and ran. Unfortunately, the kids were below the brow of the hill and couldn't see the two that ran right up the power line before diving into the balsam brush. "You just missed seeing some deer," the kids were told. But then Alex tensed and aimed his forefinger at the woods to the north. Isak's eyes followed the direction, and so did Grandpa Bob's. Two other deer were moving slowly parallel to the trail. One deer veered toward Moose Lake Road, crossed it, and vanished, but the other one walked and paused, keeping a wary eye on the kids.

"C'mon, Isak," Alex ordered, and started into the woods after the deer. The deer took a few more steps and stopped. The kids took a few steps and stopped. The deer moved some more. The kids moved some more. Then the deer broke into trot. Once more, Alex called to his smaller brother: "C'mon, Isak!" and started running.

With that, the deer bounded out of the woods and ran down the power line, Alex in hot pursuit. Isak's short legs didn't allow him to leap over windfalls like his brother, but he kept churning along through the understory as Alex and the deer dashed on ahead. Finally tiring of the game, the deer bounded off at high speed. Alex, realizing he wasn't going to catch the animal, stopped on the power line. Isak came crashing out of the woods and stopped. They both stared into the brush where the deer had so recently vanished. Then they took off for the house to tell Grandma Edith about their adventure. The deer will never know it, but he made the day for a couple of little kids.